HAL LEONARD BANJO METHOD BOOK 2

SECOND EDITION

For 5-String Banjo

BY MAC ROBERTSON, ROBBIE CLEMENT, AND WILL SCHMID

ISBN 978-0-7935-2813-4

HAL•LEONARD®
CORPORATION

7777 W. BLUEMOUND RD. P.O. BOX 13819 MILWAUKEE, WI 53213

In Australia Contact:
Hal Leonard Australia Pty. Ltd.
4 Lentara Court
Cheltenham, Victoria, 3192 Australia
Email: ausadmin@halleonard.com.au

Visit Hal Leonard Online at
www.halleonard.com

CONTENTS

INTRODUCTION

Book 2 of the *Hal Leonard Banjo Method* is a continuation of the banjo basics and techniques learned in Book 1. The material in Book 2 not only reinforces and strengthens Book 1 instruction, but it also features:

- More **solos** and standard **licks**

- **Melodic-style** banjo

- **Fiddle tunes**, such as "Devil's Dream" and "Bill Cheatham"

- Playing **back-up**

- Use of the **capo** and more **music theory**

LET'S PLAY

Let's get right down to it! "New River Train" is a bluegrass standard. After you have learned the words and melody, play the banjo part which includes familiar techniques from Book 1.

NEW RIVER TRAIN

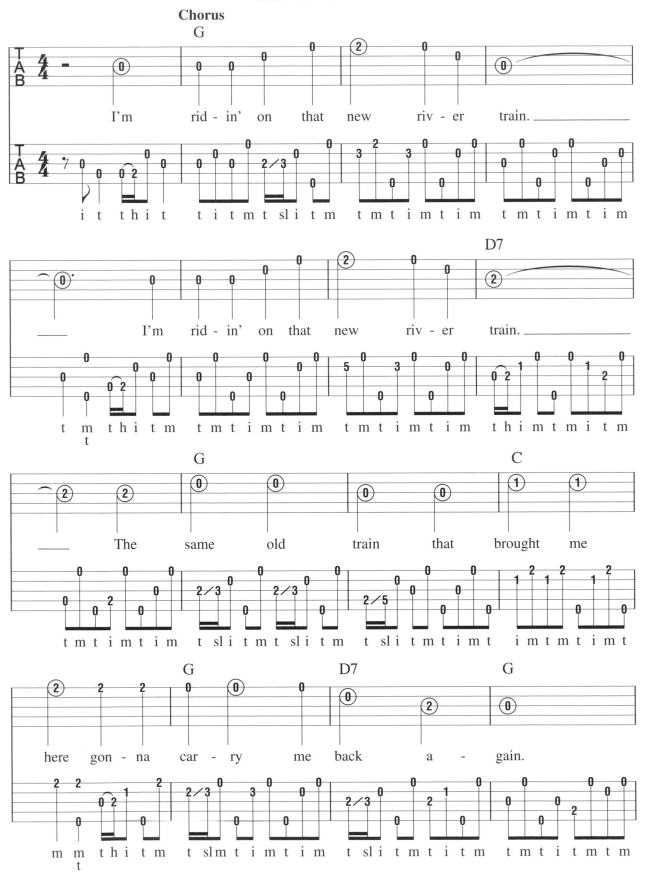

Verse

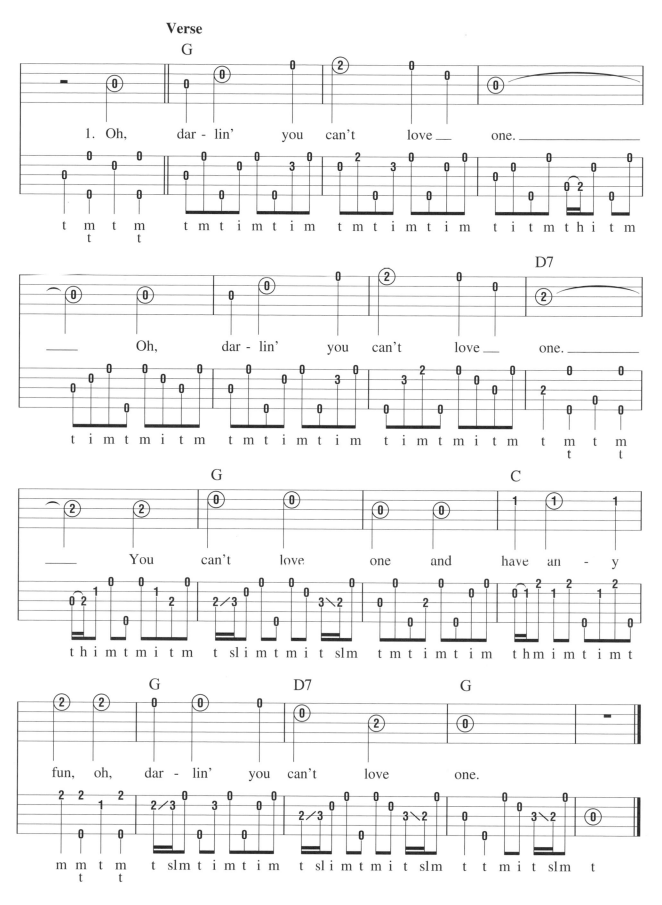

2. You can't love two and still be true.

3. You can't love three and still love me.

4. You can't love four and love me anymore.

5. You can't love five and long survive.

6. You can't love six, you'll run out of tricks.

7. You can't love seven and still go to heaven.

FORWARD & FORWARD-BACKWARD ROLL

The first four notes of this new roll come from the forward roll, and the last four notes are taken from the forward-backward roll. This new combination roll is used in the arrangement of "The Cuckoo."

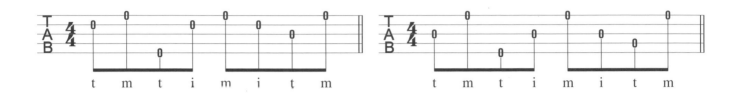

THE CUCKOO

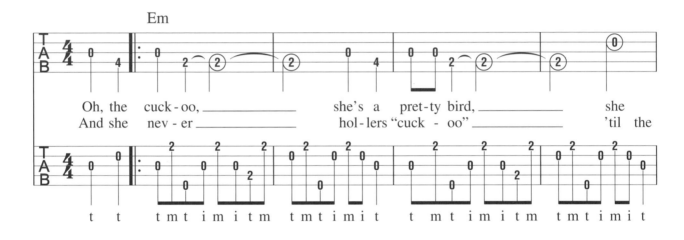

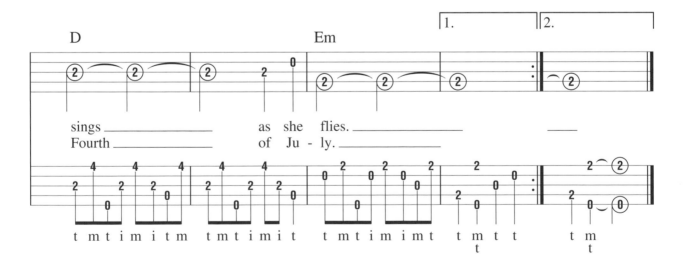

The banjo part to "Down the Road" gives you another chance to practice the new combination roll.

First play the melody, then practice the banjo part emphasizing the melody notes.

DOWN THE ROAD

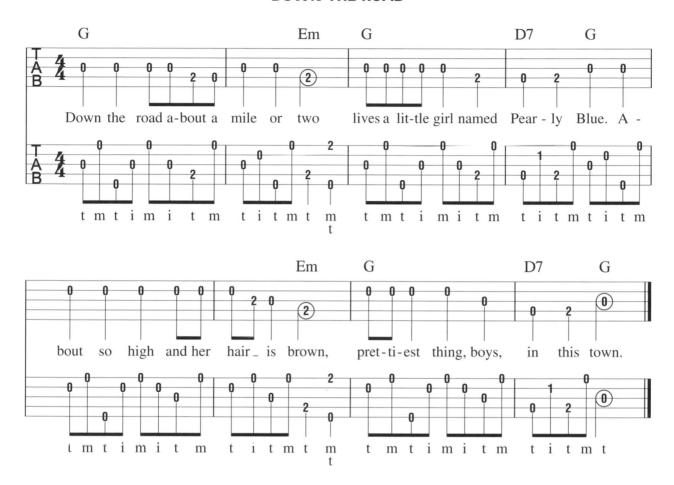

"Goin' Down the Road" on page 9 includes two standard licks that are based on the new right-hand roll. The roll pattern alone looks like this for the first lick:

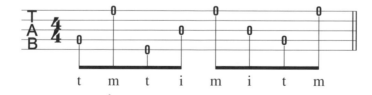

Now use the second finger to fret each second-fret note.

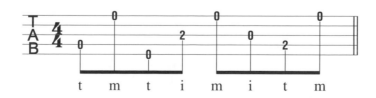

Then add a slide to produce the complete lick. This pattern appears as a fill-in lick in measure 8.

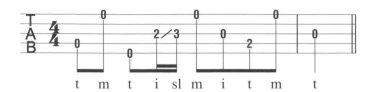

The second lick is based on this roll pattern:

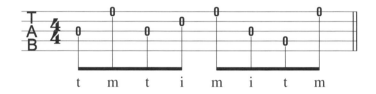

Use the second finger again to fret the second-fret notes.

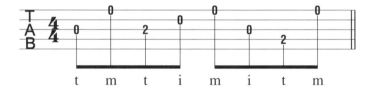

Then add a slide. This lick appears as an ending in measure 16:

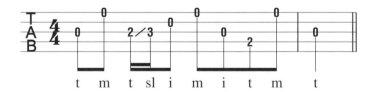

Measure 3 includes this new pattern. Use the second and third fingers of the left hand as indicated to play these notes:

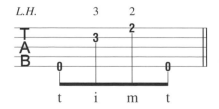

Play the melody first, then try the banjo arrangement paying special attention to the rhythm of the introduction and the left-hand fingering in measure 3. ‎ǂ indicates an eighth rest.

GOIN' DOWN THE ROAD

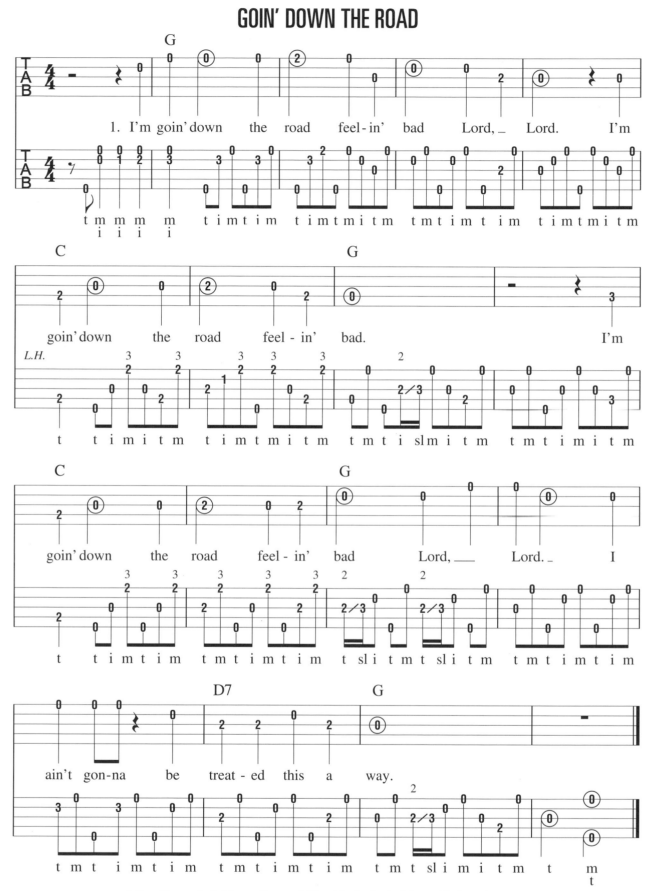

2. I'm goin' where those chilly winds don't blow. (3 times)
   I ain't gonna be treated this a way.

3. I'm goin' where the water tastes like wine. (3 times)
   I ain't gonna be treated this a way.

4. I'm goin' where the climate suits my clothes. (3 times)
   I ain't gonna be treated this a way.

The next song uses the new chord, C7. Study the diagram, then play the chord. Check the strings by strumming one at a time to make sure each rings clearly.

A dot behind a note increases its value by one half. Thus ♪., equals ♪ ♪ or three beats.

After you have learned the melody to "In the Pines," practice the C7 chord by strumming as you sing the song. After you are familiar with the melody and chords, add the accompaniment part.

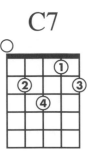

C7

IN THE PINES

continue accompaniment

2. Little girl, little girl, what have I done
    That makes you treat me so?
    You've caused me to weep, you've caused me to mourn,
    You've caused me to leave my home.

10

The banjo part to "Bury Me Beneath the Willow" includes this variation of the new right-hand roll. Practice the example before playing the song.

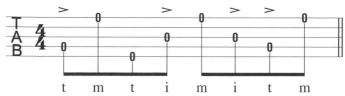

In measures 3 and 11 the melody is played on the second fret of the third string while the left hand is playing a C chord. Move the second finger from the fourth string to the third string to play the melody note, then move it back to its usual position.

BURY ME BENEATH THE WILLOW

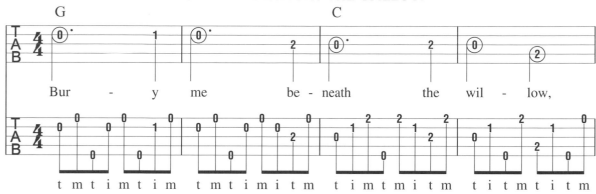

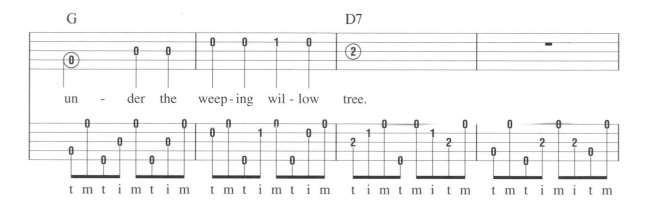

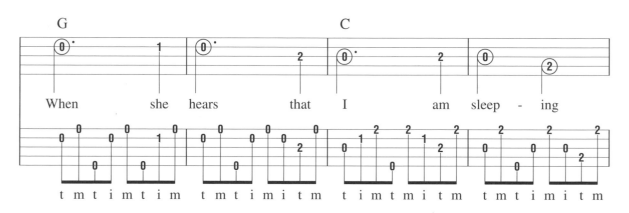

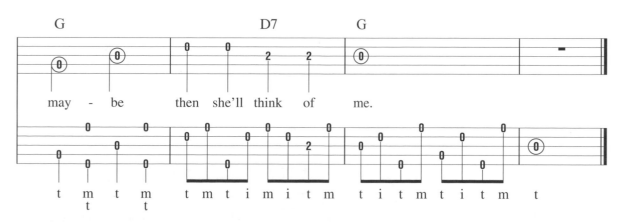

Bur - y me be - neath the wil - low,

un - der the weep-ing wil - low tree.

When she hears that I am sleep - ing

may - be then she'll think of me.

11

The banjo part to "Froggy Went A-Courtin'" includes the two new licks you have just learned. Locate them in measures 3 and 15, and practice them separately before playing the whole arrangement.

FROGGY WENT A-COURTIN'

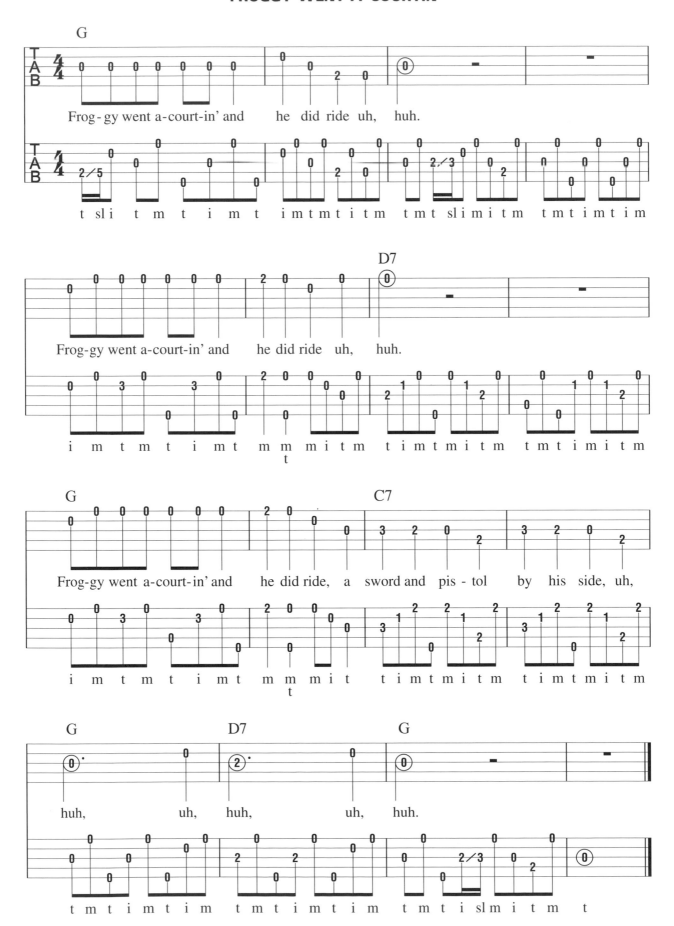

MELODIC BANJO

THE G MAJOR SCALE

Throughout Book 1 you have played the banjo in G tuning. Most of the melodies (the top line of tablature) have ended on the G chord and used notes which are part of the G **major scale**.

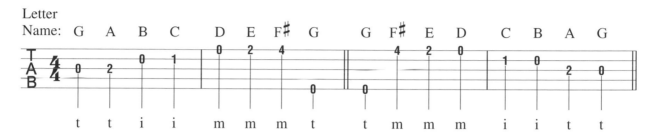

A scale is named by the first and last note. The major scale has a specific pattern of whole and half steps which is undoubtedly familiar to your ear. When a melody is based on such a scale and has a tonal center of G, that melody is in the **key** of G major. Most melodies in the key of G major end on the note G.

Alternate Fingerings for Notes

Most notes can be played in several different places on the banjo fingerboard. Compare the sound of these two notes. Both sound the note A.

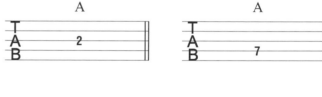

Now play this three-note pattern both ways. The left-hand fingering (L.H.) is indicated above the note.

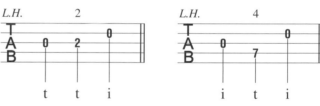

The new **melodic banjo style** you are about to study employs alternate fingerings to allow the right hand to pick faster and each note to ring longer. Follow the indicated left- and right-hand fingerings carefully as you play "Merrily We Roll Along" using this new method.

MERRILY WE ROLL ALONG

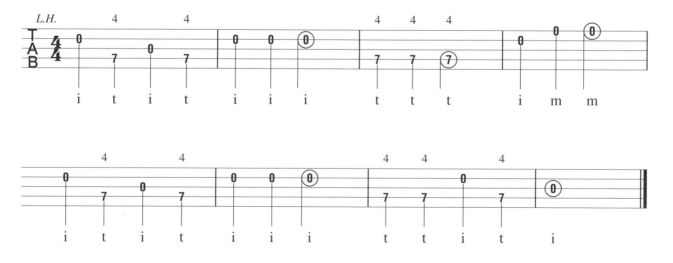

The note C can also be played in a different position. Compare these two versions of the first five notes of the G scale.

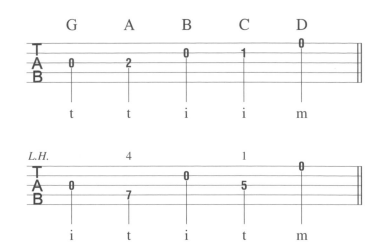

Now play "Aunt Rhody" using the new fingerings. Notice the right-hand middle finger (m) in measure 4.

AUNT RHODY

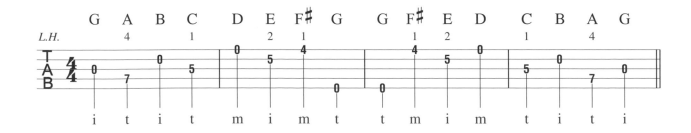

MELODIC EXERCISES

Two ways of playing the note E are:

Now combine all of these fingerings to play the complete G major scale. Practice the scale many times until you can play it smoothly; then go on to the exercises on the next page.

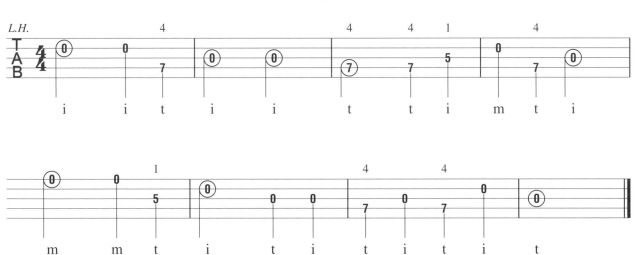

The left-hand fingers will be placed in one of two positions as you play the following exercise.

(measures 1 and 7)   (measures 3 and 5)

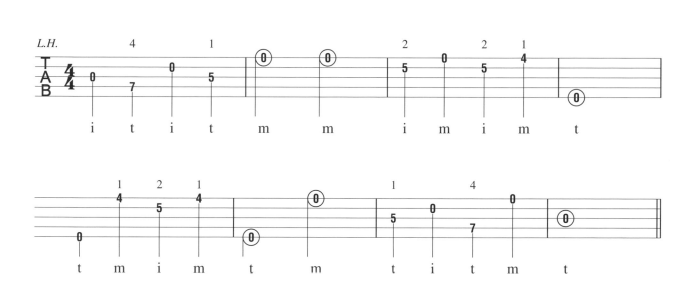

Watch the indicated fingerings closely as you play the next song. This exercise should be played slowly at first even though it uses eighth notes.

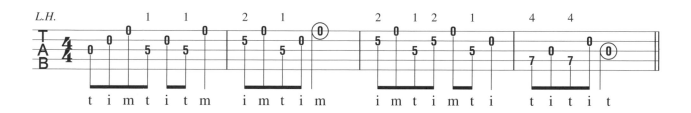

FIDDLE TUNES

These new fingering patterns make it possible to play many kinds of melodies. Melodic banjo style combines these new patterns with standard bluegrass techniques to play fiddle tunes. There are thousands of these lively tunes that fiddlers play at dances. Some were passed from one musician to another for many years before they were collected and published. Others are recent compositions.

Fiddle tunes often consist of an eight-measure melody called the **A Part** which is played twice and another eight-measure melody called the **B Part** which is also played twice.

"The Devil's Dream" is a popular traditional fiddle tune played in melodic banjo style. Since the melody line and banjo part are the same, only a single line of tablature is necessary. The tune is played twice in a row on the CD; first slowly, then at full speed.

Watch the fingering carefully as you play the tune. The second note (F#) is played at the seventh fret of the second string rather than the fourth fret of the first string for the same reasons we have adopted the other new fingerings—it allows quicker right-hand picking and more sustained tones.

The bracket under the series of notes in measures 3 and 4 indicates that you should hold all the fingers down as if you were playing a chord. This occurs again in measures 11 and 12.

THE DEVIL'S DREAM

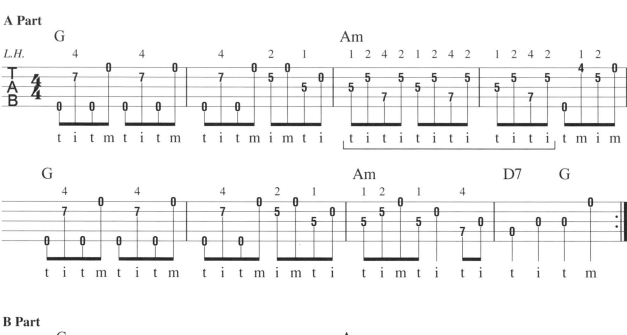

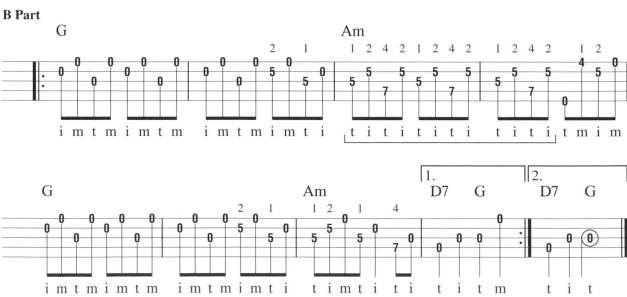

SLIDE VARIATIONS

The rhythm of left-hand techniques may be changed to achieve different musical effects.

This familiar slide pattern was introduced earlier:

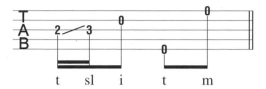

The first three notes of this pattern are played in three steps:

1. Pick the third string with the thumb.

2. Slide the middle finger of the left hand from the second to third fret.

3. Pick the open second string with the index finger of the right hand.

The rhythmic notation indicates two sixteenth notes played in the space of one eighth note. This rhythm could be altered so that the slide is delayed and arrives at the same moment the open second string is played.

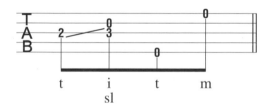

The first three notes are now played in only two steps:

1. Pick the third string with the thumb.

2. Slide the middle finger from the second to third fret so that it arrives at the same time the open second string is picked.

The rhythm of the slide has been lengthened from a sixteenth note to an eighth note. Notice the different sound produced by this change in the rhythm.

"Cotton-Eyed Joe" is presented below with three banjo parts. After you are familiar with the melody and words, play the first version which uses sixteenth-note slides.

COTTON-EYED JOE

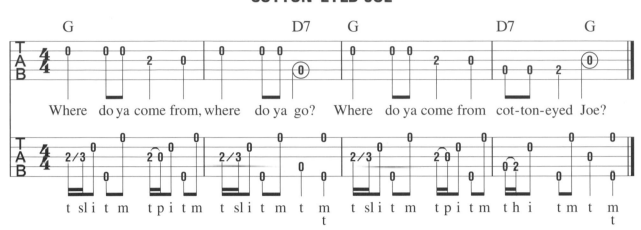

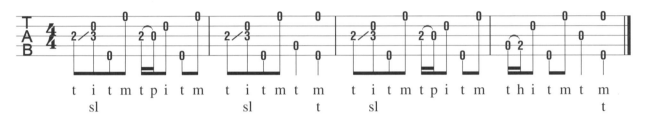

The second version uses the eighth-note slides.

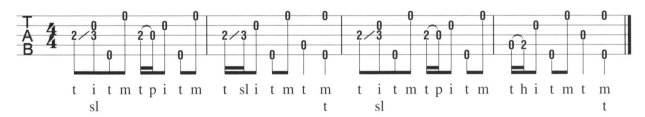

The third version uses both slide rhythms.

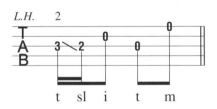

Practice the following slide patterns which appear in the banjo arrangement of "Old Dan Tucker" on the next page.

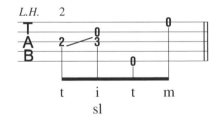

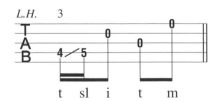

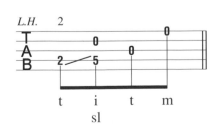

OLD DAN TUCKER

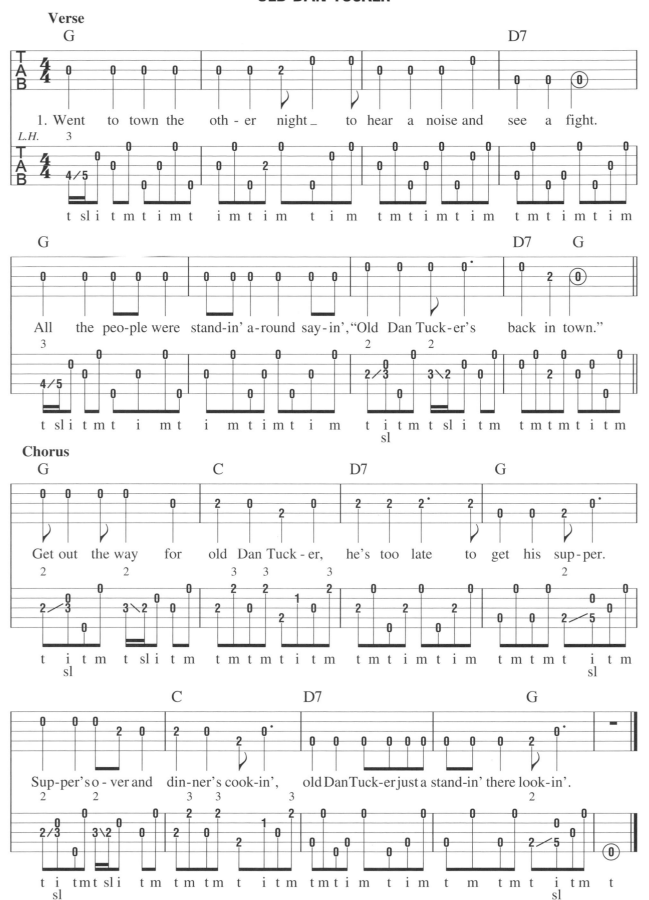

2. Old Dan Tucker's a fine old man,
Washed his face in a frying pan.
Combed his hair with a wagon wheel,
Died with a toothache in his heel. *CHORUS*

This song features a variety of chord changes. The fingering for the B7 chord in measure 11 is given on the Chord Chart, page 64.

PALLET ON YOUR FLOOR

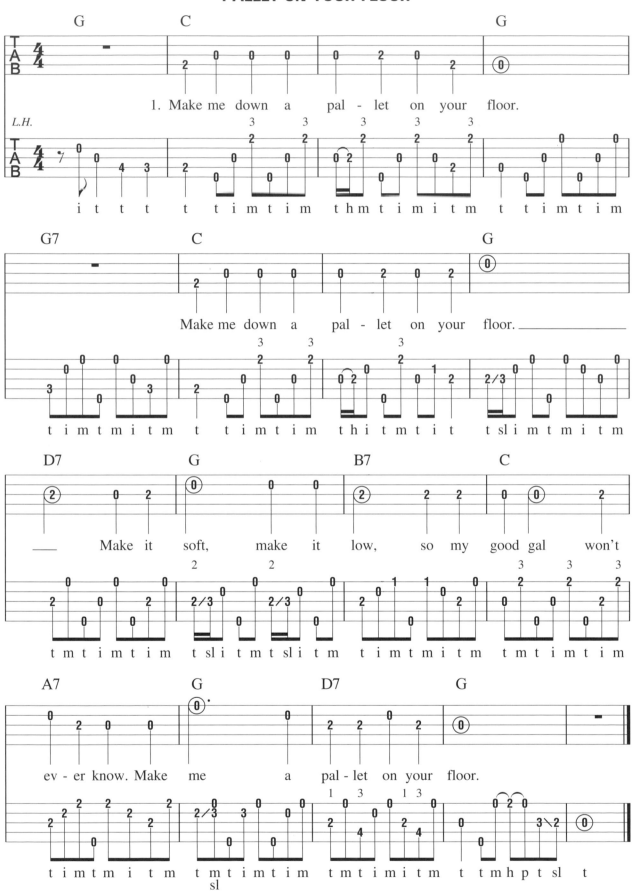

2. Hello all you good time friends of mine.
   Hello all you good time friends of mine.
   When I had a dollar you treated me so fine,
   Where are you when I only need a dime?

3. Never drive a stranger from your door.
   Never drive a stranger from your door.
   Someday you may be a stranger too,
   Never drive a stranger from your door.

"Railroad Bill" is another traditional blues tune like "Pallet on Your Floor," which also includes a B7 chord. The first measure of the banjo part includes a new variation of the forward roll. Practice the example before you play the song.

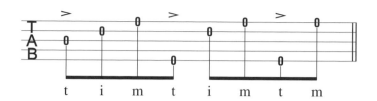

RAILROAD BILL

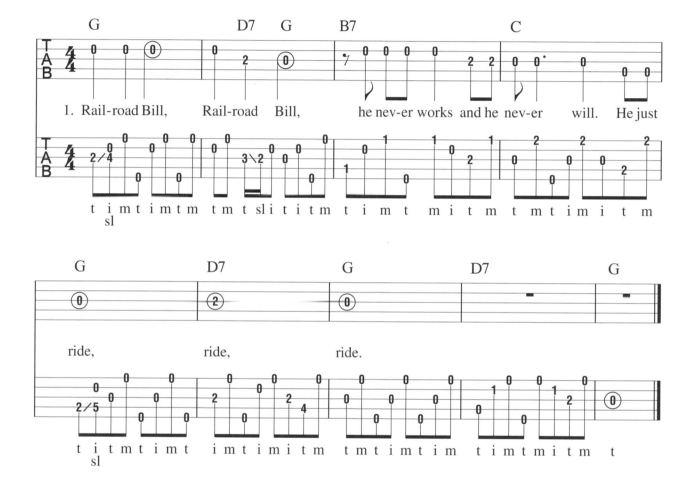

1. Rail-road Bill, Rail-road Bill, he nev-er works and he nev-er will. He just ride, ride, ride.

2. Kill me a chicken, send me the wing,
   Think I'm workin', I don't do a thing.
   Just ride, ride, ride.

3. Railroad Bill, Railroad Bill,
   Live way up on Railroad Hill.
   Just ride, ride, ride.

NEW HAMMERS & PULLS

So far, the hammer-on has been played starting with an open string. It is possible to hammer-on from one fretted note to another.

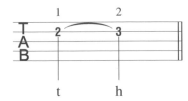

Here are some examples of this new hammer-on. Be sure to use the correct left-hand fingering shown above the tab.

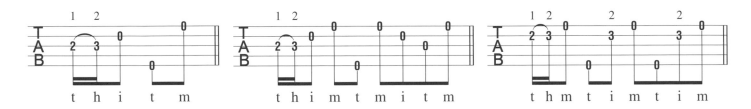

Now try this exercise using the new hammer-on:

The pull-off can also occur from one fretted note to another. Play the following example using the left-hand fingers shown. The first finger must be pressed down firmly as the second finger pulls off.

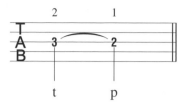

Try these patterns which use this pull-off:

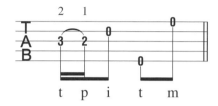

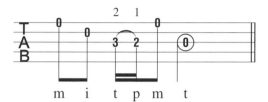

The following exercises use the new hammer-on and pull-off. Notice how they are combined with the forward-backward roll in measure 3 of the bottom exercise. This common bluegrass lick also appears in measure 4 of the next song.

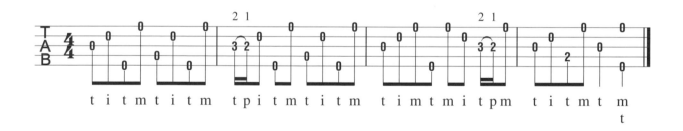

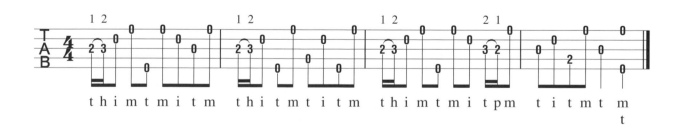

Watch for the whole notes as you play the melody to "Sittin' on Top of the World." The banjo part includes the new hammer-on and pull-off patterns in measures 2, 4, 10, and 16.

SITTIN' ON TOP OF THE WORLD

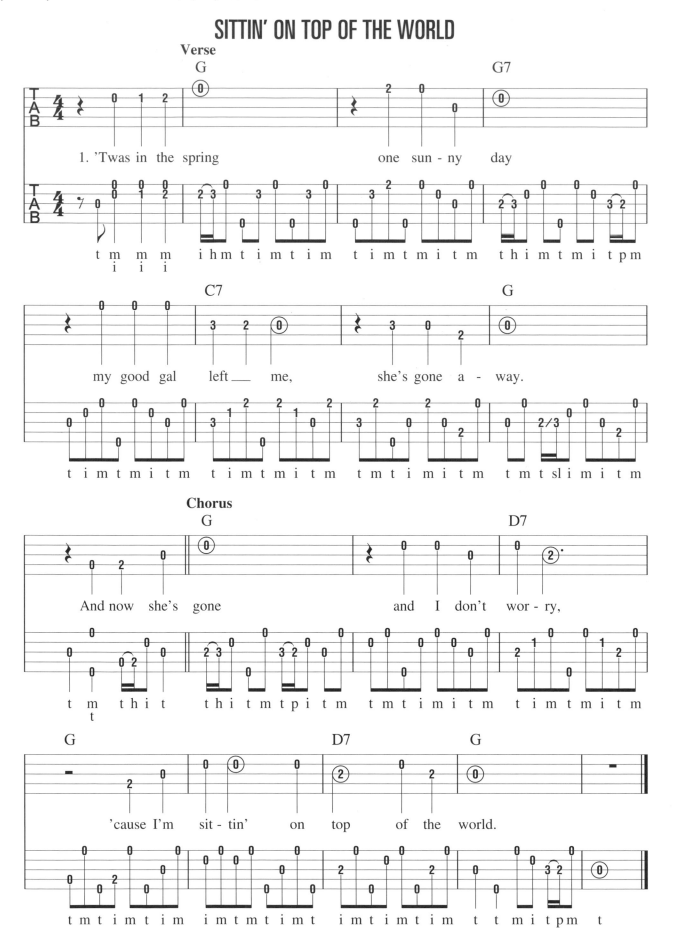

2. She called me up from down in El Paso,
   Said "Come back, Daddy, I need you so." *CHORUS*

3. Mississippi River runs deep and wide,
   The woman I'm loving is on the other side. *CHORUS*

"The Girl I Left Behind" is another traditional fiddle tune arranged for melodic banjo style. The tune is very old and may have been played during the Revolutionary War.

You will need to add three notes on the fourth string to the melodic G scale you learned earlier. Practice the scale both ascending and descending until you can play it smoothly.

Now play the banjo arrangement paying special attention to the indicated fingerings.

THE GIRL I LEFT BEHIND

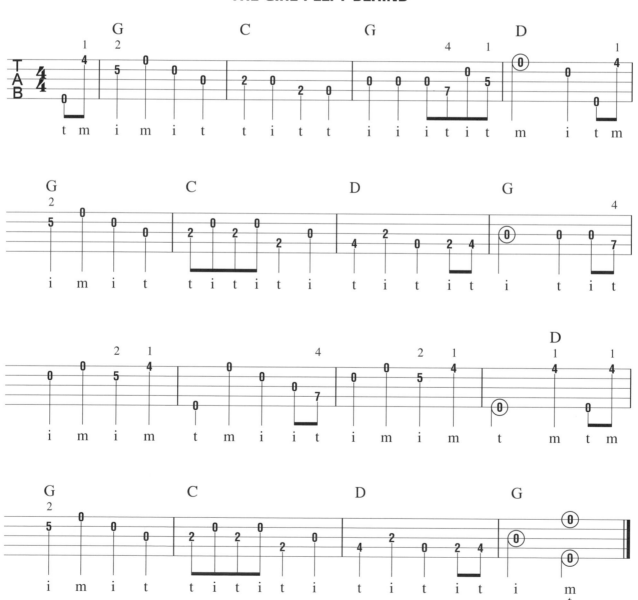

Here's another great song featuring slides and the new hammer-ons and pull-offs.

LITTLE MAGGIE

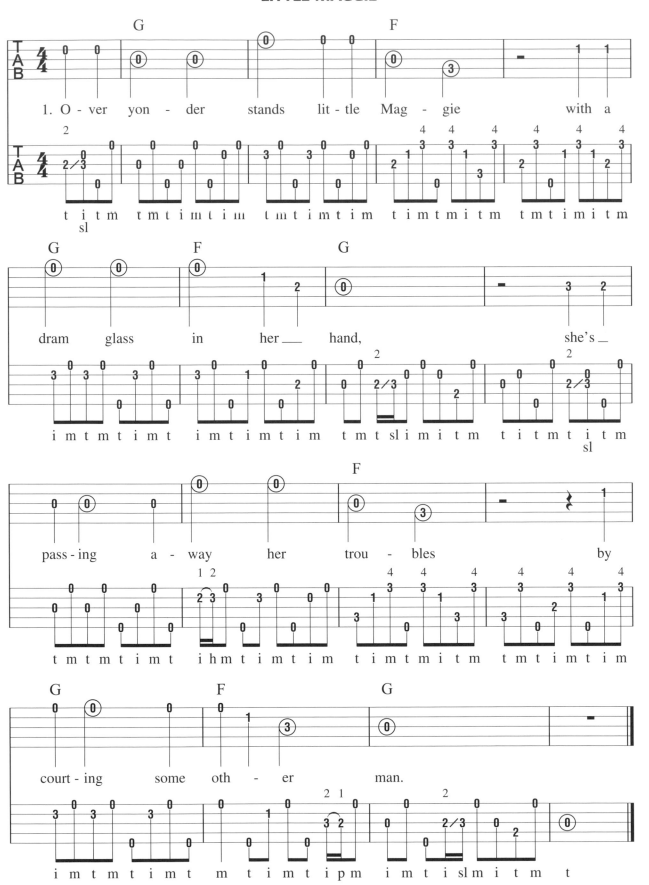

2. Oh, how can I ever stand it
Just to see them two blue eyes,
A shining in the moonlight
Like two diamonds in the skies.

3. Pretty flowers were made for blooming
Pretty stars were made to shine,
Pretty women were made for loving
Little Maggie was made for mine.

4. Last time I saw little Maggie
She was setting on the banks of the sea,
With a forty-four around her
And a banjo on her knee.

PLAYING BACK-UP

Bluegrass banjo style was developed in a string band with other musicians playing at the same time. If you know someone who plays guitar, ask them to strum the chords as you play the songs you know. It is fun to play with others, and two or more instruments help fill out the sound.

You may discover that if the banjo always plays a solo part, it is likely to be much louder than the other instruments and voices. You must therefore learn to play **back-up** parts which do not interfere with someone else's instrumental solo or singing.

Many of the accompaniment patterns presented in previous songs can be used as back-up parts. Back-up parts often incorporate four-finger chords called **moveable chords** because the basic chord pattern can be moved anywhere on the fingerboard.

The F chord is a moveable chord that you already know. Moving the chord pattern up two frets produces an alternate form of the G chord.

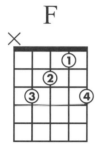

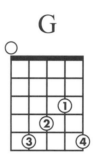

Practice the two chords by strumming "Little Maggie" on the preceding page.

An interesting back-up part may be played by using the same chords in combination with this right-hand picking pattern:

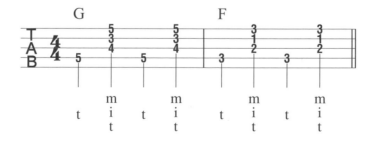

The first half of the song is presented below with the new back-up chords and picking pattern written in the banjo part.

LITTLE MAGGIE
(Back-up)

The thumb notes on beats one and three can be omitted. Play this new back-up variation for the second half of the song:

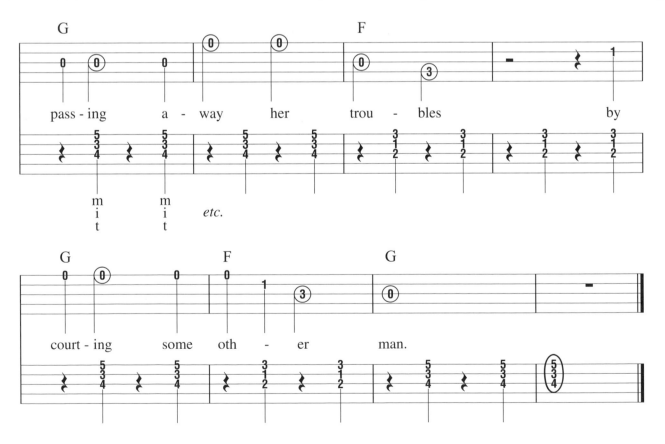

"Mama Don't 'Low" is an instrumental showpiece. The pauses at the end of the lines are often filled with flashy or "hot" licks. After you learn the melody, play the banjo part which includes licks using the new techniques you have learned.

You will notice that as more complicated licks are included, the banjo part does not follow the melody as closely as before. Be careful not to lose the melody among the other notes. Singing the melody softly or humming as you play the banjo part may help preserve the correct rhythmic accents.

MAMA DON'T 'LOW

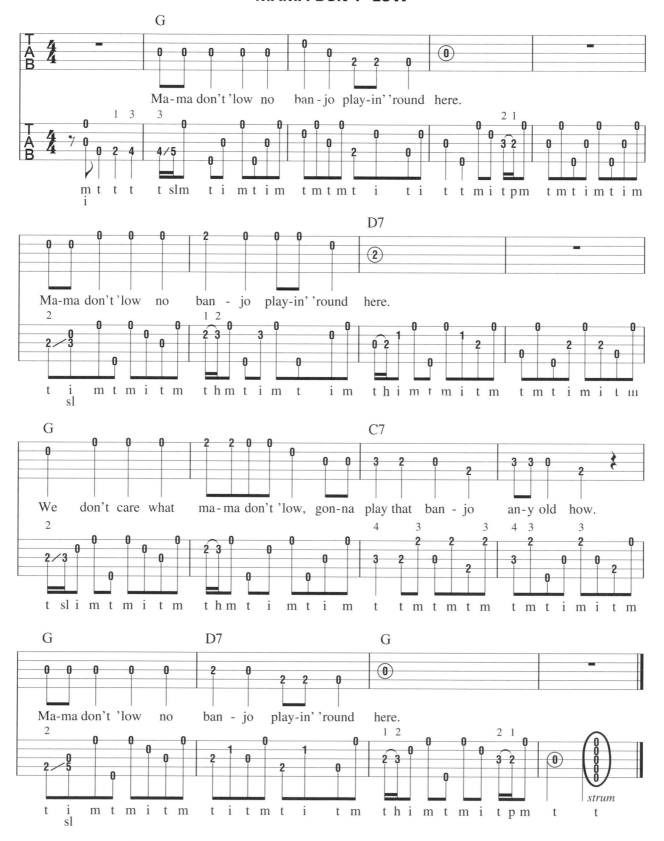

"Guitar" or any other instrument could be substituted for the word "banjo" in the lyrics. Each player in a group would then be given a chance to fill in the pauses with their own solos.

"Jesse James" is a well-known outlaw ballad. It is fun to sing with a group, so be sure to learn the words and melody before going on to the banjo parts presented on the following pages.

JESSE JAMES
(Melody)

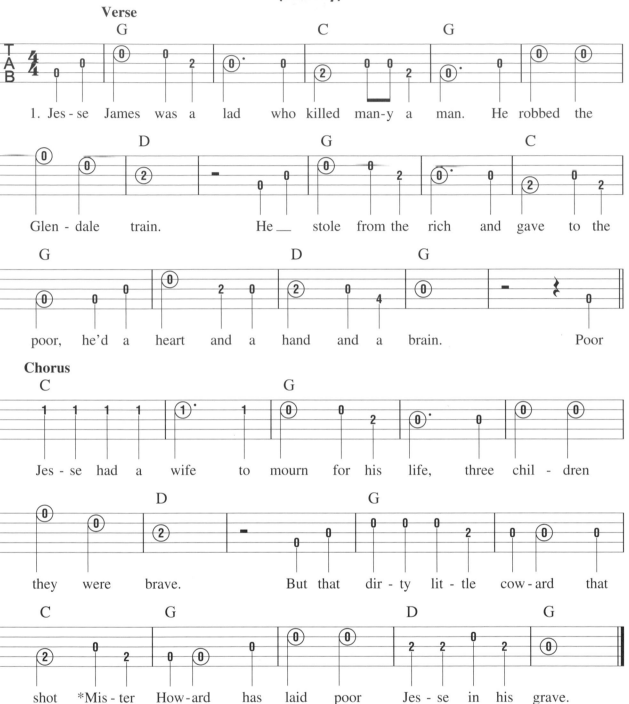

2. It was on a Wednesday night, the moon was shining bright,
They robbed the Glendale train.
And the people they did say for many miles away
It was robbed by Frank and Jesse James.

3. It was on a Saturday night when Jesse was at home,
Talking with his family brace.
Robert Ford came along like a thief in the night
And laid poor Jesse in his grave.

4. Robert Ford, that dirty little coward
I wonder how he feels.
For he ate of Jesse's bread and slept in Jesse's bed
And he laid poor Jesse in his grave.

5. This song was made by Billy Gashade
As soon as the news did arrive.
He said there was no man with the law in his hand
Who could take Jesse James when alive.

* Mister Howard was the name Jesse James assumed in later life.

When you have learned the melody to "Jesse James," you may want to add a back-up banjo part.

A new moveable form of the C chord can be played by barring the index finger across strings four through one at the fifth fret, as indicated in the diagram.

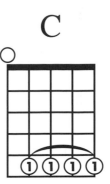

Here are the three basic forms of moveable chords that you now know.

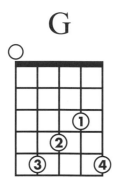 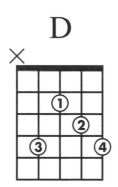 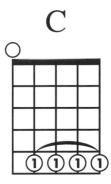

Practice these chord forms by strumming "Jesse James."

After you can change smoothly from one chord to another, try damping the strings by releasing the left-hand pressure immediately after the right-hand strums. The left-hand fingers remain in contact with the strings to stop the sound. This produces a characteristic back-up sound called a "pop" or "choonk."

Combine this new technique with the back-up banjo part below. Notice that the right hand plays on the upbeats two and four rather than the downbeats one and three. With a suitable guitar part, this produces the standard "boom-chick" back-up that is often heard.

JESSE JAMES
(Back-up)

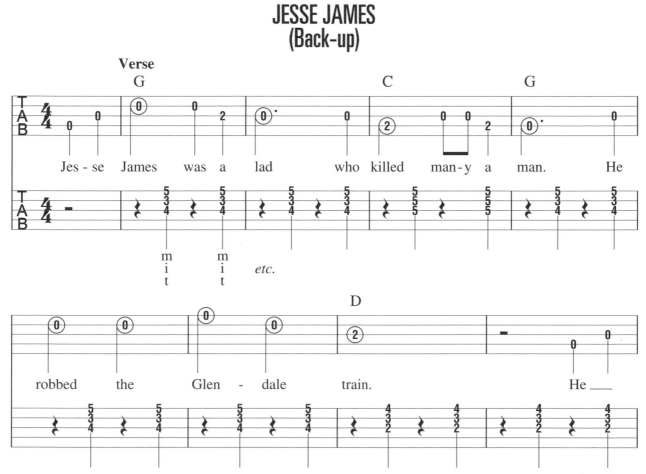

continue throughout

31

THE PUSH-OFF & OTHER TECHNIQUES

It may be more convenient to play a left-hand pull-off by pushing the finger away from the palm of your hand (toward the ceiling) rather than pulling it in toward the palm. This is especially true on the third and fourth strings or when the finger that has just pulled off must fret a new note on the lower string. Use a push-off to play these examples:

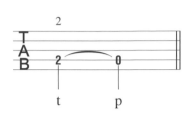 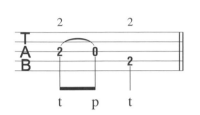 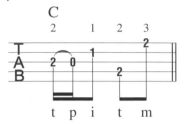

Measures 4, 11, 12, and 28 of the banjo part contain patterns that could be played with either a push-off or pull-off. Try both techniques and use the one that works best for you.

JESSE JAMES
(Banjo Solo)

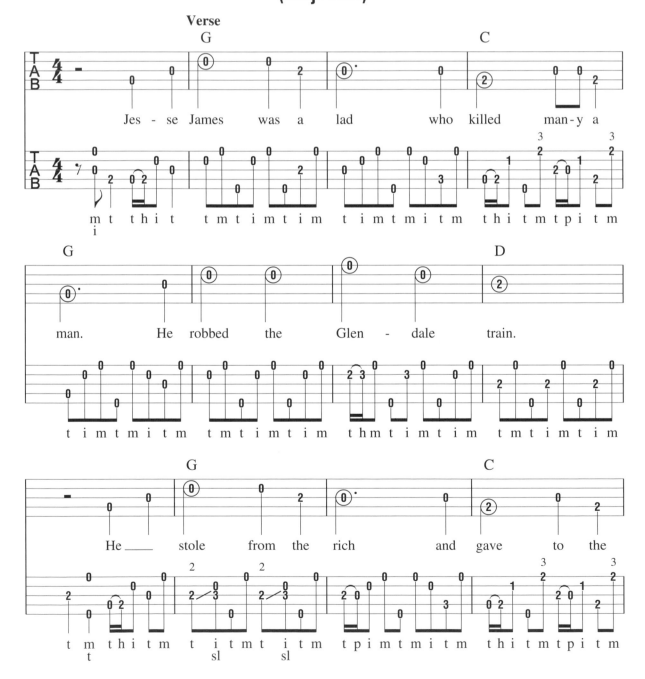

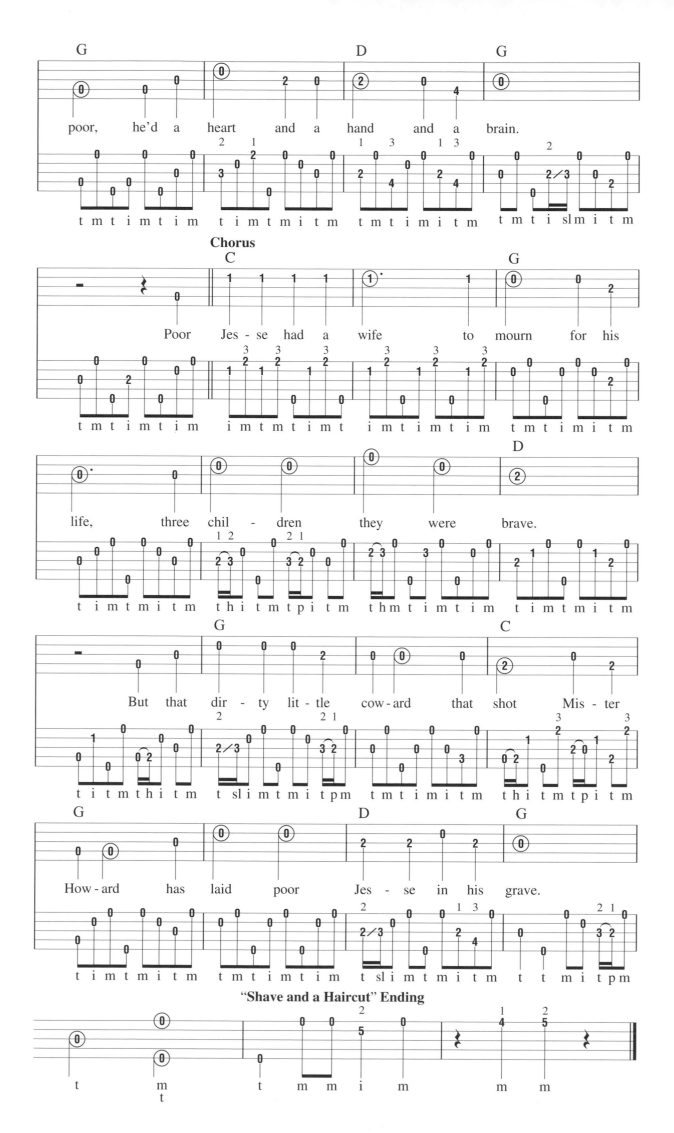

33

This famous tune features a new right-hand pattern.

OH, SUSANNA

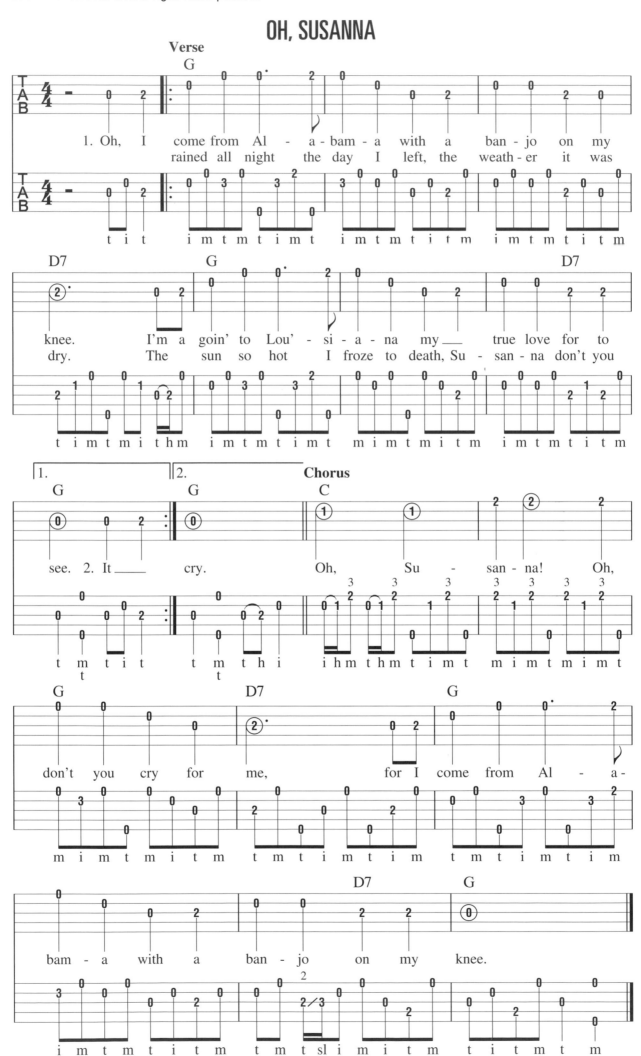

"Cumberland Gap" includes the following new left-hand slide pattern in measures 2 and 6:

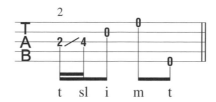

CUMBERLAND GAP

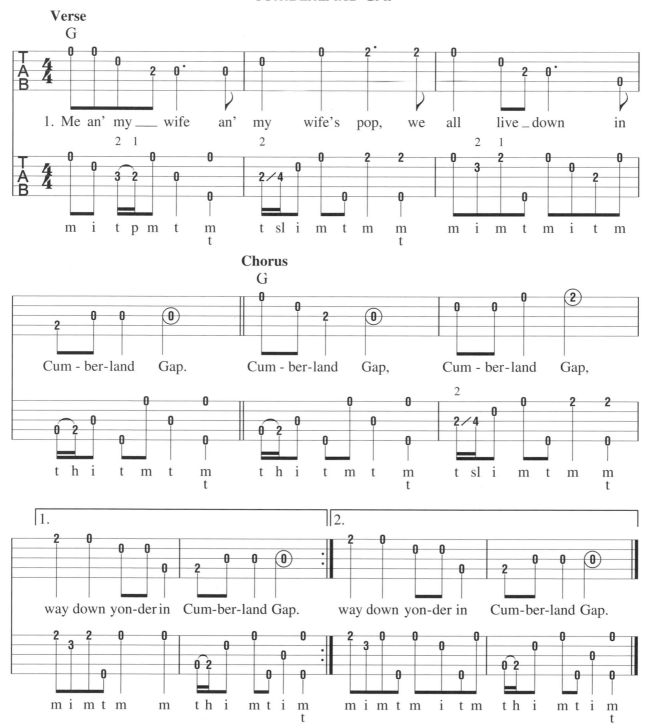

2. Cumberland Gap is a fine old place,
   Three kinds of water to wash your face.

3. Daniel Boone with his old flintlock,
   Shot him a bear on Pinnacle Rock.

4. Lay down boys and take a little nap,
   Dream about a place called Cumberland Gap.

An eighth-note pull-off may replace a note in the right-hand roll. Watch for this substitution as you play the banjo solo to "Hard, Ain't It Hard."

HARD, AIN'T IT HARD

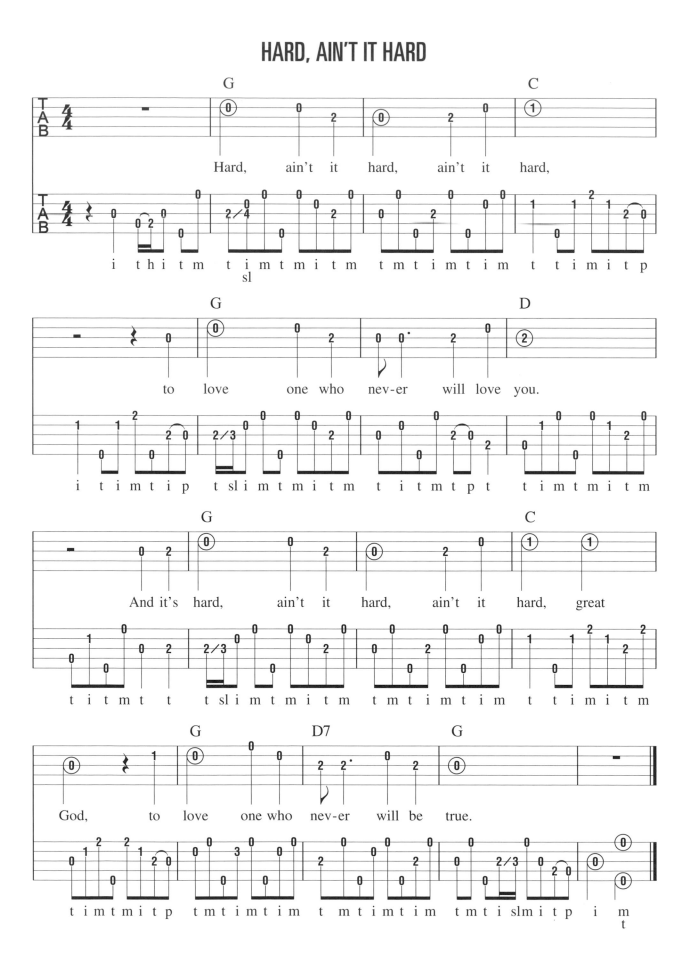

Gospel songs have always been an important part of bluegrass music. An eighth-note hammer-on replaces a right-hand roll note in measure 6 of the banjo part. Measure 15 contains a new ending lick. Watch the suggested fingerings closely as you play the banjo part.

DO LORD

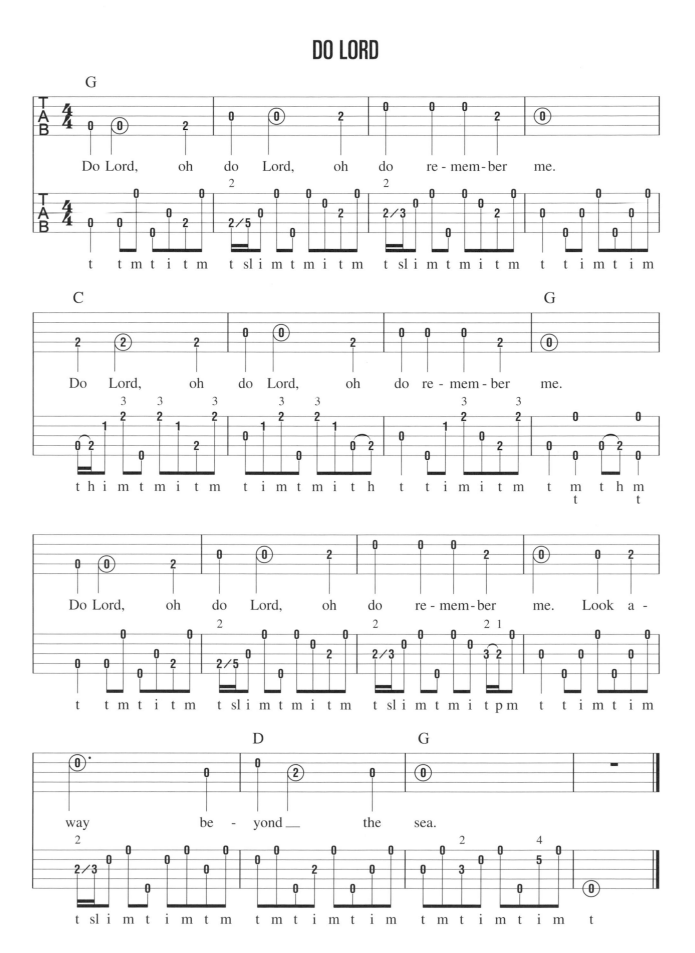

The banjo part to "Lonesome Valley" includes an eighth-note hammer-on combined with a right-hand roll in measure 16. Both the left- and right-hand notes sound at the same time.

LONESOME VALLEY

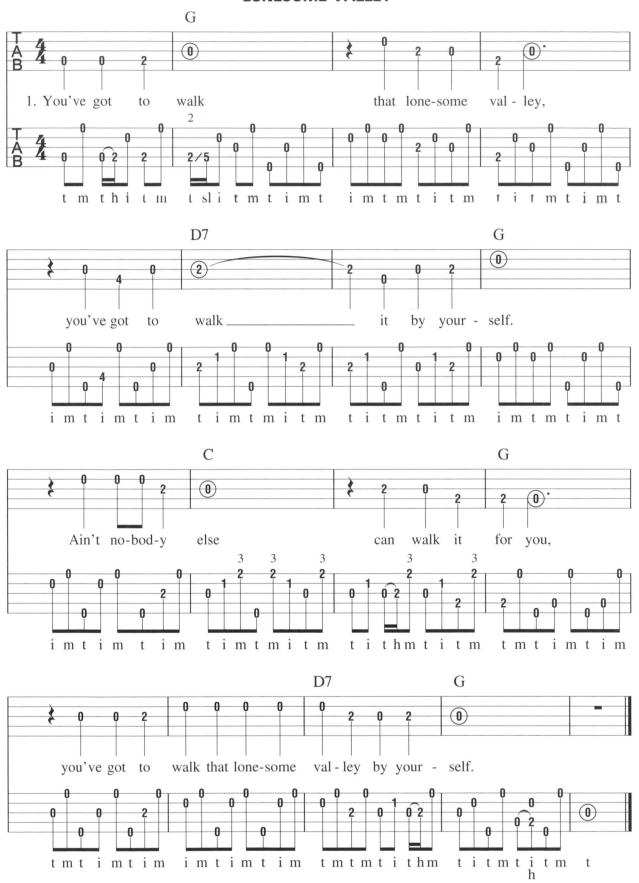

2. Your sister's got to walk that lonesome valley...

3. Your brother's got to walk that lonesome valley...

4. We've all got to walk that lonesome valley...

THE BACKWARD ROLL & OTHER PATTERNS

The **backward roll** is based on this right-hand finger pattern:

Notice that the right-hand fingers move across the strings from 1–5 when playing this pattern.

Practice this basic backward roll before playing the banjo accompaniment to "Skip to My Lou."

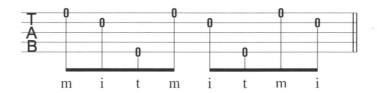

SKIP TO MY LOU

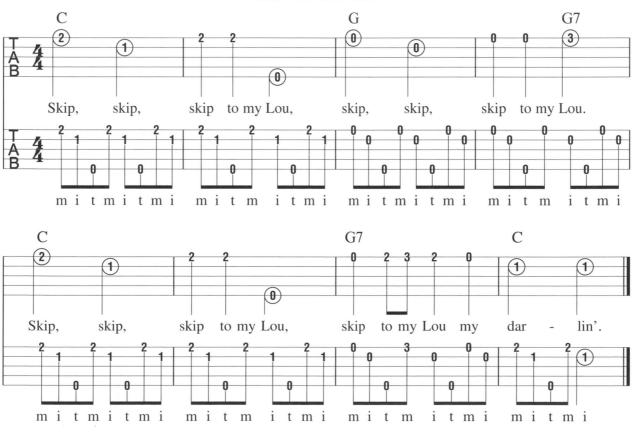

The backward roll is especially useful when the melody notes are on the first string. Notice how the backward roll is used in the banjo part of "Way Down Town."

WAY DOWN TOWN

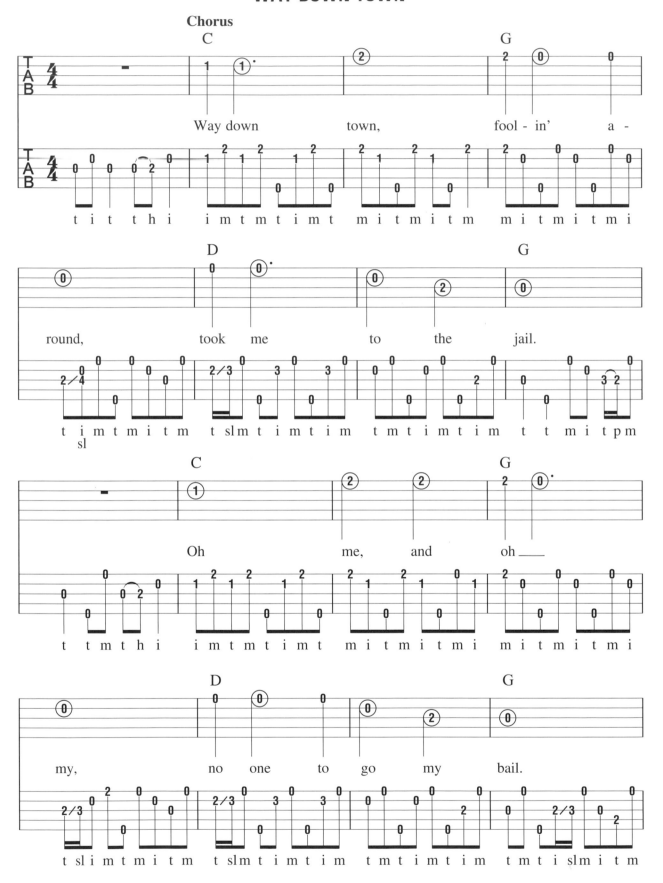

Verse

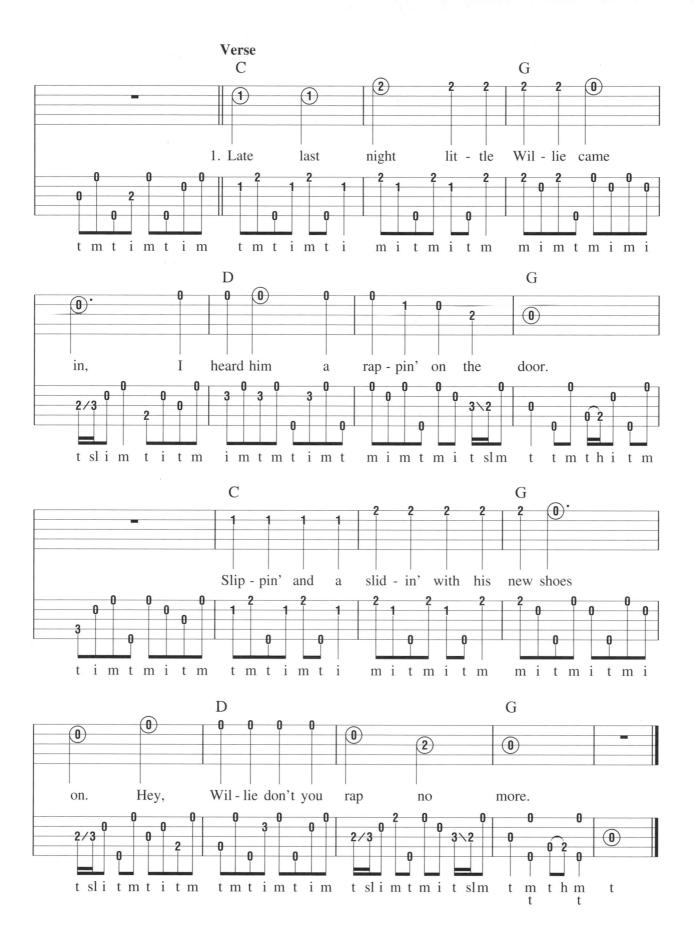

2. I wish I was over at my little Rosy's house,
   Sittin' in a big arm chair.
   One arm around this old banjo,
   The other around my dear. *CHORUS*

3. One old shirt is about all I've got,
   A dollar is what I crave.
   Brought nothin' with me into this old world,
   Ain't gonna take nothin' to my grave. *CHORUS*

"John Hardy" is a famous outlaw ballad often used as an instructional showpiece. As you learn the melody, notice the four distinctive melody notes that occur during each pair of C chord measures. Keep the full C chord in place during these measures and add the fourth finger to the third fret of the first string as indicated here:

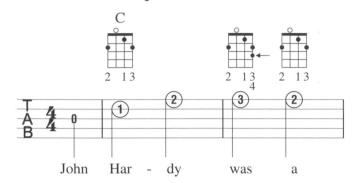

JOHN HARDY
(Melody)

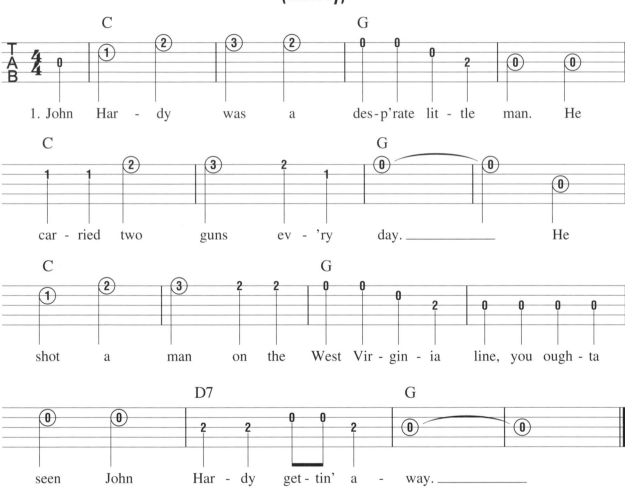

2. John Hardy went out on the Freestone Bridge,
   Where he thought he'd be free.
   Up stepped the deputy with a gun in his hand,
   Said "Johnny come and go with me."

3. John Hardy had a mother and a father,
   He sent for them to come and go his bail.
   There was no bail allowed for the murderin' man,
   So they locked John Hardy back in jail.

4. John Hardy had a pretty little girl,
   The dress she wore was blue.
   She came to the jail with a loud, loud shout,
   Sayin', "Johnny I been true to you."

5. John Hardy was a standin' in his cell,
   The tears was a rollin' down his eyes.
   He said, "I been the death of many a poor boy,
   And now I'm ready to die."

6. "I been to the East, I been to the West,
   I been this wide world around.
   I been to the river and been baptized,
   So take me to the hangin' ground."

The banjo solo for "John Hardy" that appears below is different for each pair of C chord measures, although the melody notes are the same. Any melody may be played several different ways.

Practice measures 4 and 8, which include licks using the eighth-note hammer-on and pull-off in new ways, then play the entire solo.

JOHN HARDY
(Banjo Solo)

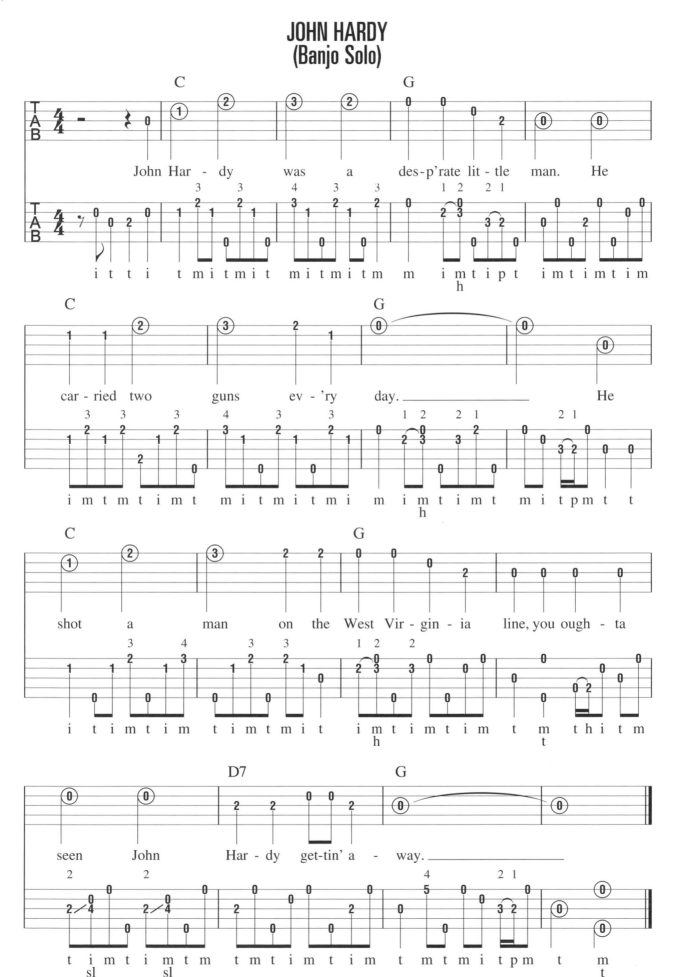

"The Eighth of January" is a traditional fiddle tune which became popular when lyrics were added to create "The Battle of New Orleans."

This melodic arrangement of the tune is based on the G scale. Practice the scale pattern until you can play it smoothly using the indicated fingerings.

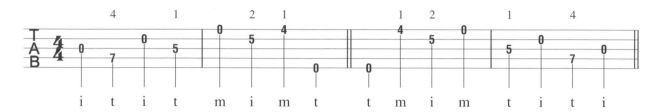

A recurring pattern requires the left hand to move quickly from the second fret to the seventh fret on the fourth string. Use the first and fourth fingers as indicated in the practice example.

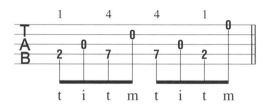

Now play the tune. Always practice at a slow, even tempo until you can play the entire piece without an error.

THE EIGHTH OF JANUARY

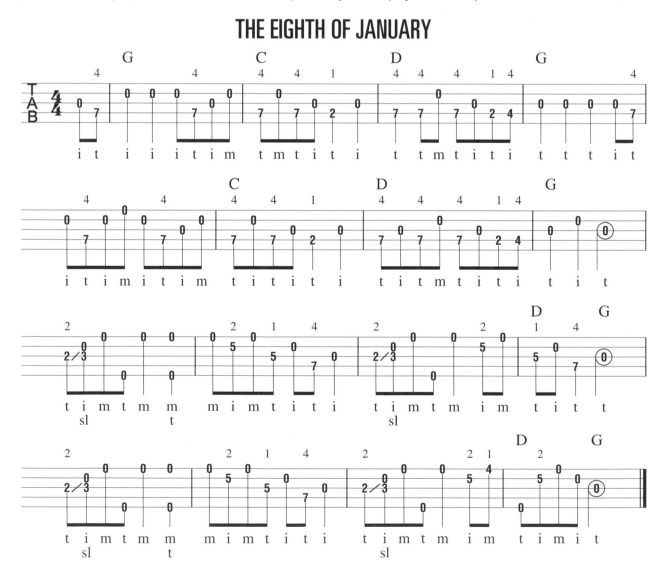

"Miss McLeod's Reel" is another fiddle tune that is presented in melodic banjo style. A new right-hand picking pattern is required in the second half of measures 9 and 13. Practice this exercise before playing the tune:

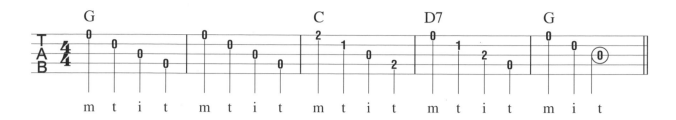

MISS MCLEOD'S REEL

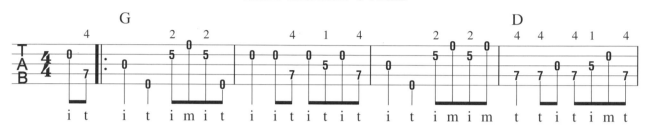

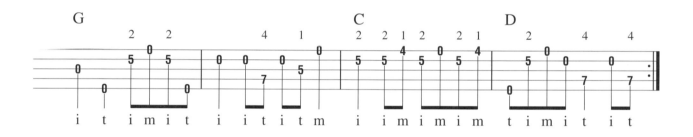

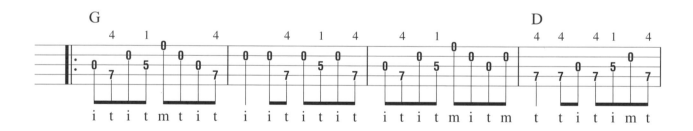

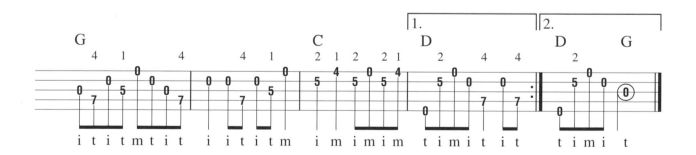

The back-up to "Crawdad" uses a new moveable chord, G7, in addition to chords previously introduced in this book. Notice that the left-hand index finger barres the first and second string to make the G7 chord.

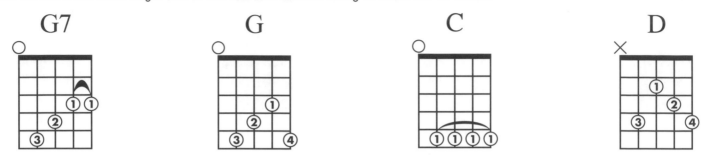

Play this back-up part as you sing.

THE CRAWDAD SONG
(Back-up)

Notice the first note in measure 6 of the banjo solo. As the third finger frets the first string, the first and second fingers should continue to fret their respective notes. Practice this example:

Adding a pull-off on the first beat produces this pattern which appears in measure 10. The first and second fingers must firmly fret their notes throughout the measure.

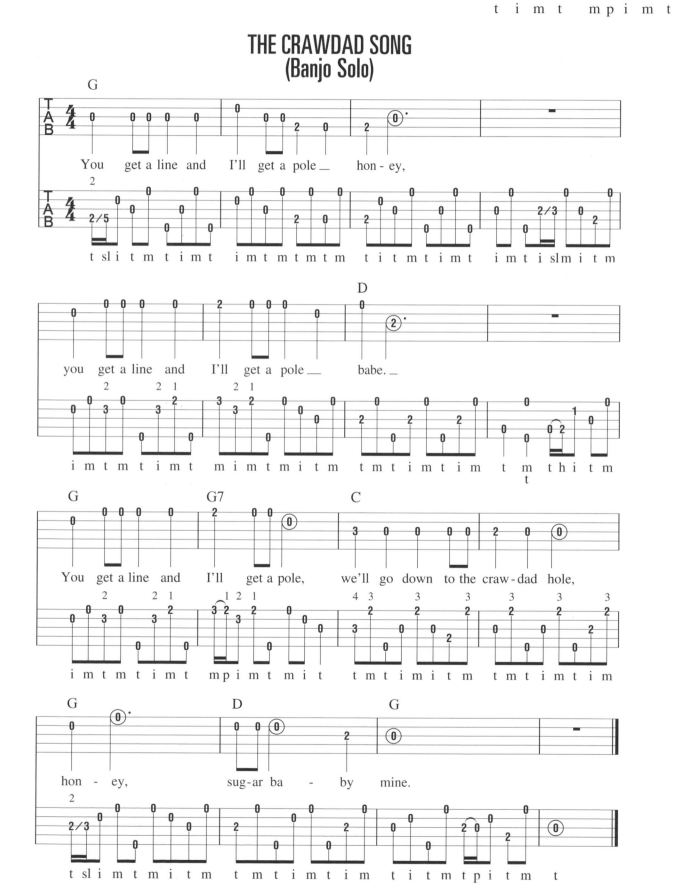

THE CRAWDAD SONG
(Banjo Solo)

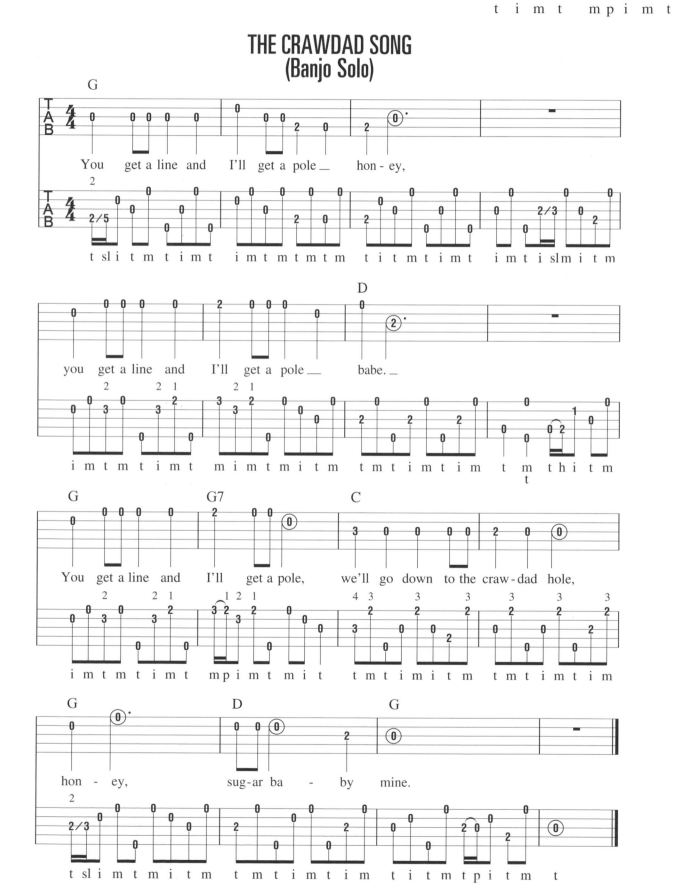

47

A new chord, D6, appears instead of the more common D7 in measure 17. This substitution is often made to add color to the banjo part. Play the chord as indicated in the diagram, then compare the sound of the D6 and D7.

Be sure to play a full C chord in measures 9 and 10. You'll then need to use the fourth finger of the left hand to fret the third-fret notes in measure 11.

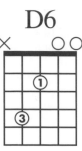

SWEET SUNNY SOUTH

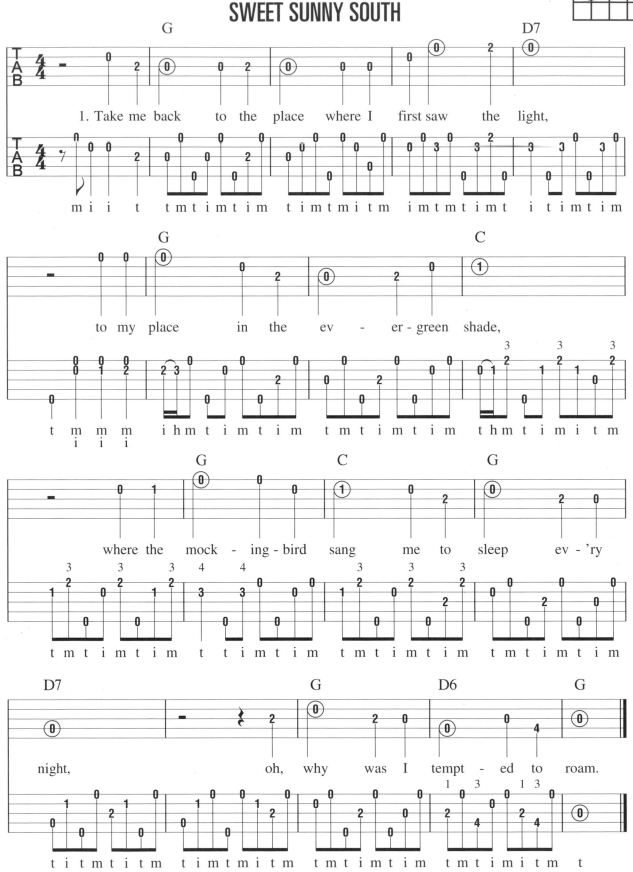

2. Take me back to the place where the orange trees grow,
   To my plot in the evergreen shade,
   Where the flowers from the river's green margin did grow
   And spread their sweet scent through the glade.

3. The path to our cottage they say has grown green,
   And the place is quite lonely around,
   And I know that the faces and the forms I have seen
   Now lie in the dark mossy ground.

"John Henry" is a classic ballad depicting the struggle between man and machine. Be sure to learn the words and melody before playing the banjo parts.

JOHN HENRY
(Melody)

2. Now every Monday morning
   When the bluebird begins to sing,
   You can hear John Henry for a mile or more.
   You can hear John Henry's hammer ring, Lord, Lord,
   You can hear John Henry's hammer ring.

3. The captain said to John Henry
   "I'm gonna bring my steam drill 'round.
   I'm gonna bring my steam drill down on the job.
   I'm gonna whop that steel on down, Lord, Lord,
   I'm gonna whop that steel on down."

4. John Henry said to the captain,
   "A man ain't nothin' but a man,
   But before I'd let that steam drill beat me down,
   I'll die with this hammer in my hand, Lord, Lord,
   I'll die with this hammer in my hand."

5. The man who invented the steam drill,
   He thought he was mighty fine,
   But John Henry drove fifteen feet.
   And the steam drill only made nine, Lord, Lord,
   The steam drill only made nine.

6. John Henry hammered in the mornin',
   His hammer was strikin' fire,
   But he hammered so hard he broke his poor heart.
   And he laid down his hammer and he died, Lord, Lord,
   He laid down his hammer and he died.

A back-up part can be added to "John Henry" using these new versions of the G and D chords:

G   7th fret

D   7th fret

Practice these new positions by strumming them as you sing, then play the back-up banjo part written below.

JOHN HENRY
(Back-up)

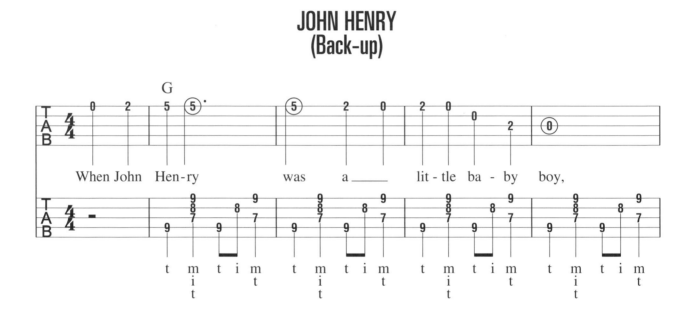

When John Hen-ry   was   a _____ lit - tle ba - by boy,

You could also damp the strings by releasing the left-hand pressure immediately after beats two and four, as indicated by the "X's."

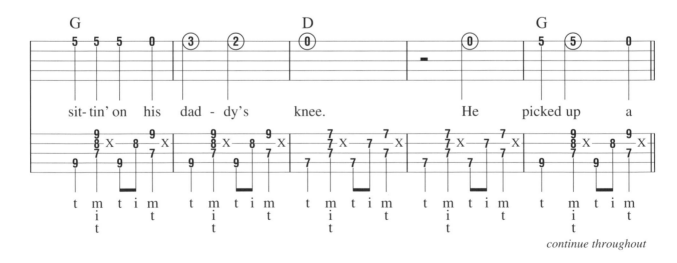

sit - tin' on   his   dad - dy's   knee.   He   picked up   a

continue throughout

The banjo solo includes most of the techniques you have learned so far. Read the tablature carefully as you play.

JOHN HENRY
(Banjo Solo)

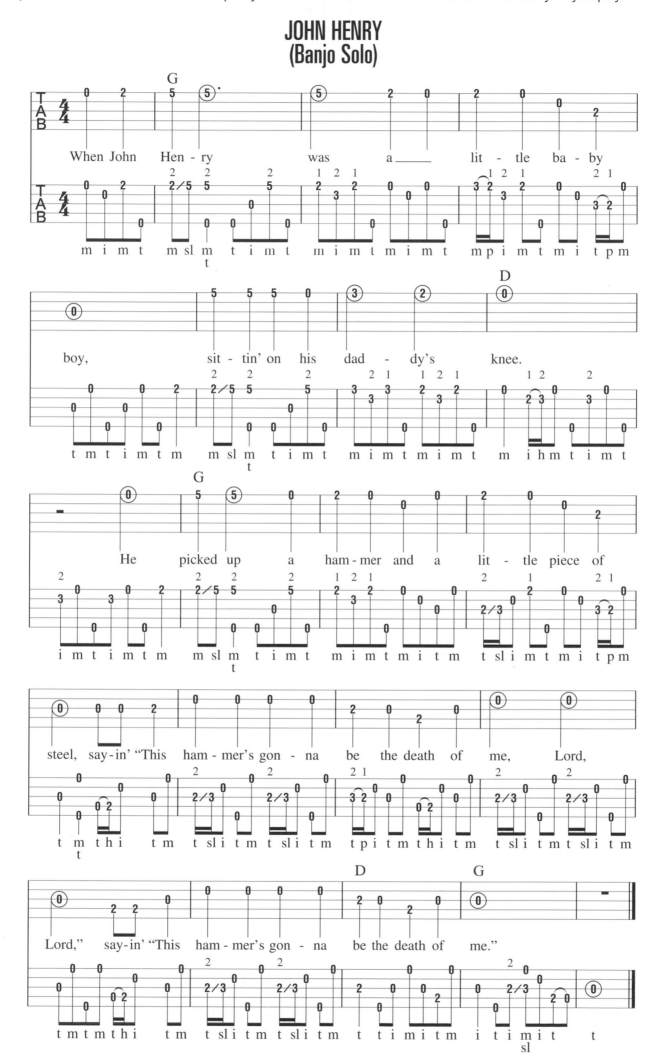

BANJO CHIMES & MORE

Banjo "chimes," or **harmonics**, are bell-like sounds sometimes used for special effects in a banjo solo. To produce this sound, lightly touch a string above the twelfth fret with the left hand without pushing down, then, strike the string sharply near the bridge with the right hand. Be sure that the left hand *does not fret* the string and is exactly above the twelfth fret wire.

In "Grandfather's Clock," all the twelfth-fret notes should be played as harmonics (H).

GRANDFATHER'S CLOCK

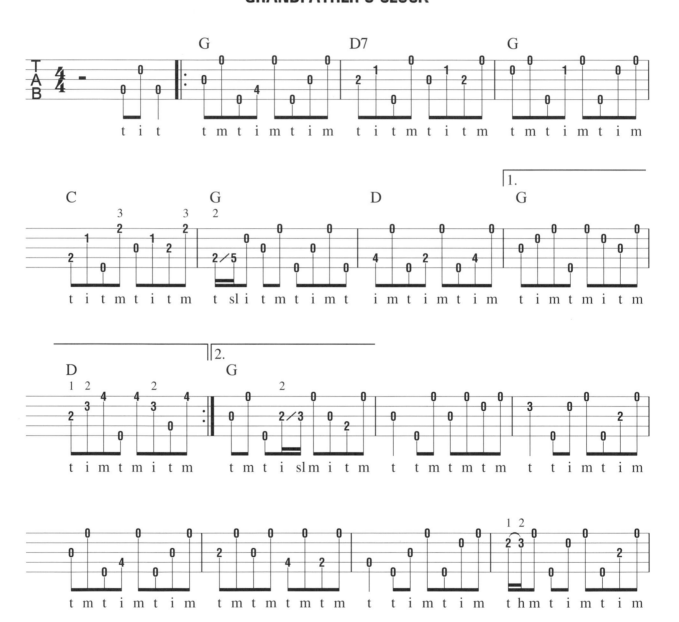

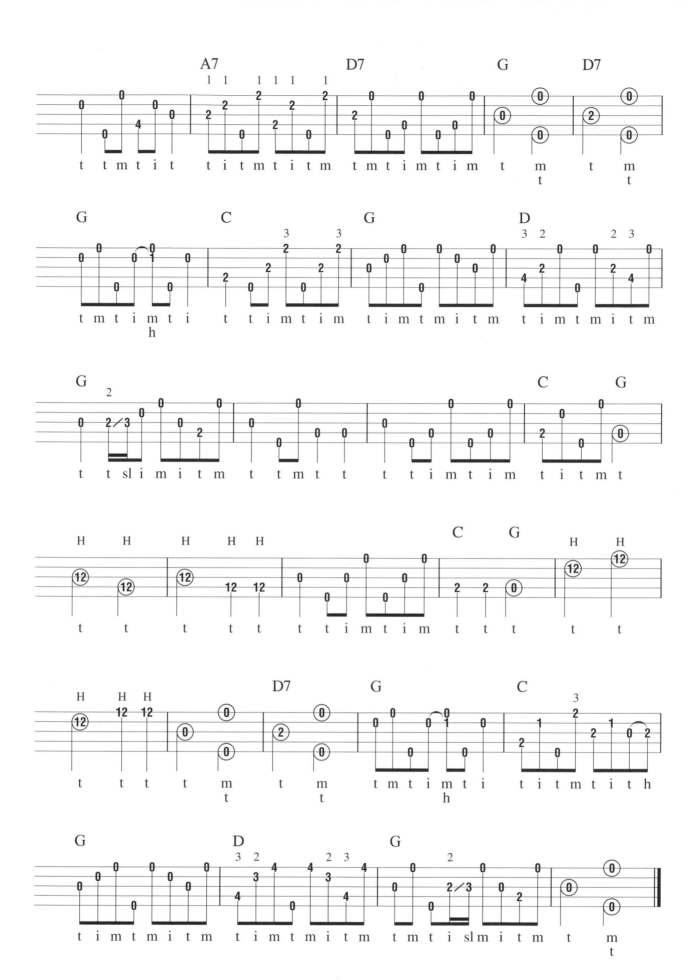

"Old Joe Clark" is a popular old-time dance tune. First, check out the melody.

OLD JOE CLARK
(Melody)

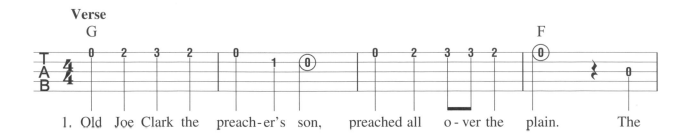

Verse

1. Old Joe Clark the preach-er's son, preached all o - ver the plain. The

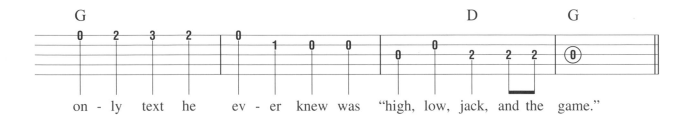

on - ly text he ev - er knew was "high, low, jack, and the game."

Chorus

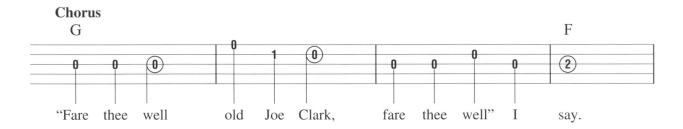

"Fare thee well old Joe Clark, fare thee well" I say.

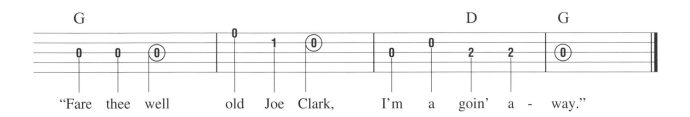

"Fare thee well old Joe Clark, I'm a goin' a - way."

2. I went down to old Joe Clark's,
   Never been there before.
   I slept on a feather bed,
   He slept on the floor.

3. Old Joe Clark he had a house
   Fifteen stories high.
   Every story in that house was
   Filled with chicken pie.

4. Wish I had a nickel,
   Wish I had a dime.
   Wish I had somebody, Lord,
   To love me all the time.

The back-up to "Old Joe Clark" uses the F chord shown below.

F

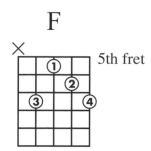

5th fret

Use this new chord along with the G and D chords from the back-up to "John Henry" to play the back-up to "Old Joe Clark."

Since the back-up for the verse and chorus are the same, only the back-up to the chorus is given.

OLD JOE CLARK
(Back-up)

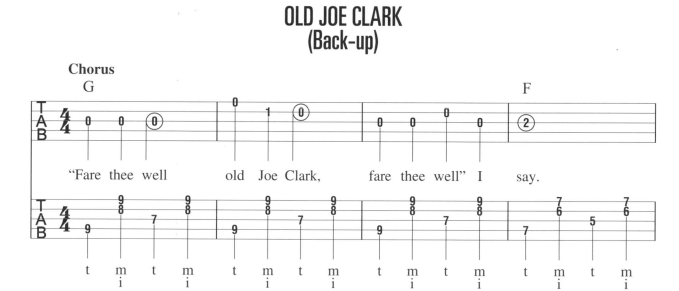

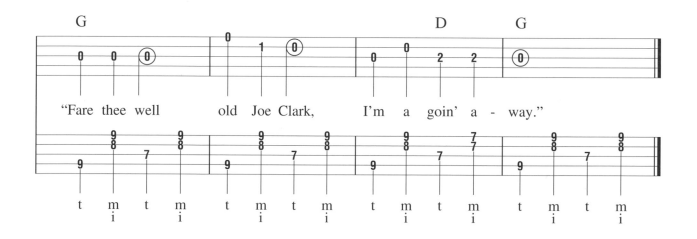

Count the rhythms slowly and carefully as you practice the banjo solo to "Old Joe Clark."

OLD JOE CLARK
(Banjo Solo)

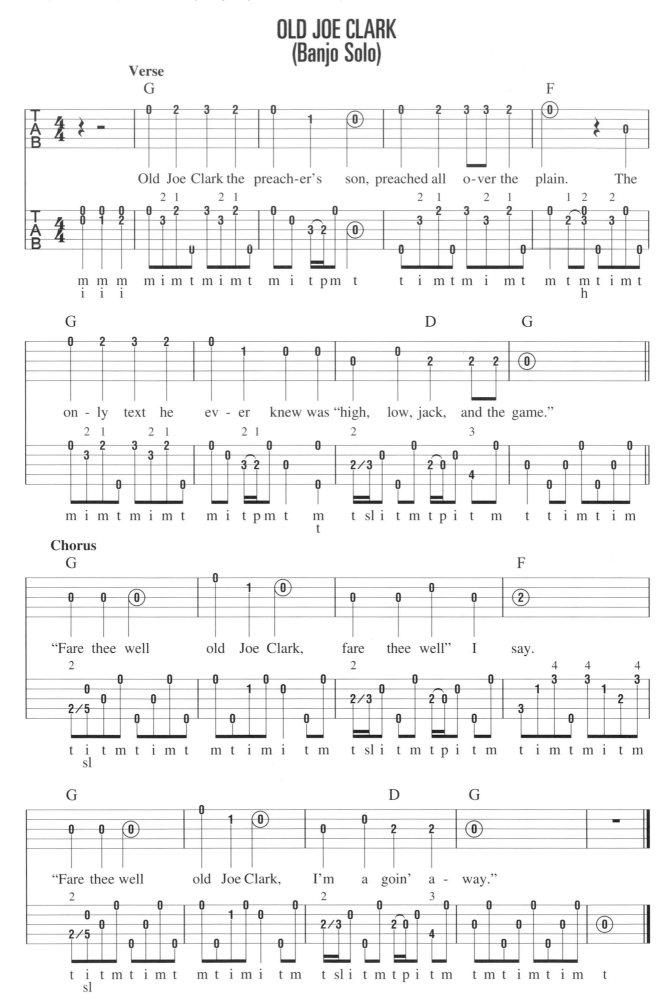

THE CHROMATIC SCALE

You have learned that adjacent frets on the banjo are one half step apart—the smallest interval between notes. A **chromatic scale** is made entirely of half steps. To play a chromatic scale, begin on the open third string and play the note at each fret from one through twelve.

The letter names of the notes are presented with the tablature below. In Book 1, you learned that the sharp (♯) raises the note one half step and that the flat (♭) lowers a note one half step.

Notice that the note between each regular letter can have two different names. The note between G and A is G♯ or A♭. The sharp is used when *ascending*; the flat is used when *descending*. Notice also that there is no note between E and F or B and C. Study this arrangement of notes and letter names carefully.

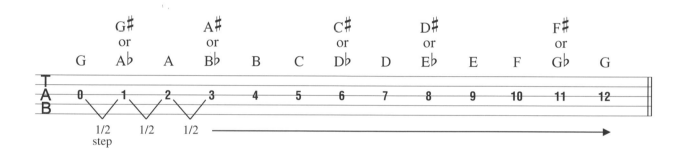

TRANSPOSING

Throughout most of Book 1 and 2, you have played songs in the **key of G**. It is called the key of G because the tonal center (most often the last note of a song) is G and because the scale on which the melodies are based is the G major scale (see page 13).

Sometimes it is helpful to raise the key to accommodate either the voice or another instrument, such as the fiddle. The process of changing the key is called **transposing**.

THE CAPO & BEYOND

A **capo** is a clamp device that can be used to mechanically transpose a song. Several varieties are available, but all have a bar that frets the strings wherever the capo is positioned on the banjo neck.

Shubb   Dunlop   Suspender

Placing the capo at the first fret raises the pitch of the notes by one half step. If you strum the open strings for what would normally be a G chord, a G♯ chord will sound. A C chord pattern will now sound as C♯.

Placing the capo at the second fret raises all the notes one whole step. An open G chord now sounds as an A chord; a C formation actually sounds as a D chord.

The capo allows you to continue playing familiar finger patterns and chords in the key of G while transposing the sound to higher keys.

What chord would sound if you strummed an open G chord with the capo placed at the fourth fret? Examining the chromatic scale on the previous page indicates that a G chord raised four half steps will become a B chord.

The most common transpositions for the 5-string bluegrass banjo are to A (2nd fret), B (4th fret), and C (5th fret). Fiddlers and mandolin players particularly like to play in A.

You will also need a separate capo on the fifth string to raise it the same number of frets that the four long strings have been raised. One option is tiny spikes placed in the fingerboard at the seventh, ninth, and tenth frets. The fifth string is then hooked under the spikes and thus fretted at the nearest fret.

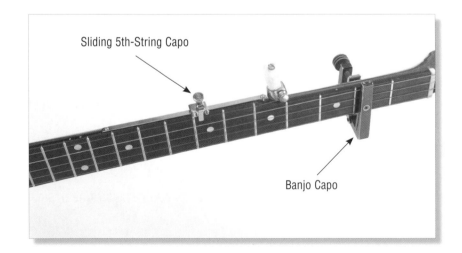

Sliding 5th-String Capo

Banjo Capo

An alternate choice is a sliding fifth-string capo. The best kind has a thumb screw rather than a spring, which tends to weaken with use. No matter which method you choose, it should be installed by a trained repairman.

When you have all your capo equipment ready, go back and try some of your favorite tunes in A or B.

"Bill Cheatham" is a favorite fiddle tune of dancers and performers. This melodic-style arrangement uses a new left-hand position in addition to the G scale presented earlier. Practice this new fingering which appears in measures 1, 2, 5, and 6.

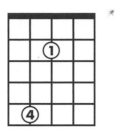

Both "Bill Cheatham" and "Soldier with a Wooden Leg" are written in the key of G, but most fiddlers prefer to play them in the key of A. Placing a capo at the second fret and raising the fifth string the same amount allows you to play the tune as written, but it will sound in the fiddler's key of A.

BILL CHEATHAM

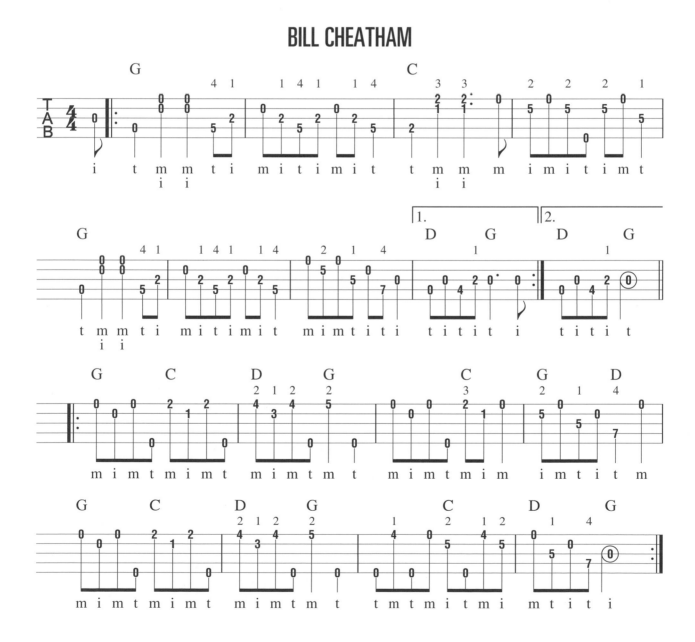

"The Little Beggarman" is based on a special kind of scale called a **mode**. The diagram below indicates that the notes are the same as a G major scale except for the seventh step, which is an *F-natural* rather than *F-sharp*. This changes the distance between scale steps and gives the tune a modal sound that is different from a tune based on the conventional major scale. This is called the **Mixolydian mode**.

Mixolydian Mode

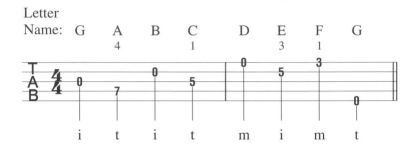

Practice the mode until you can play it smoothly, then play the tune.

THE LITTLE BEGGARMAN
(or The Red-Haired Boy)

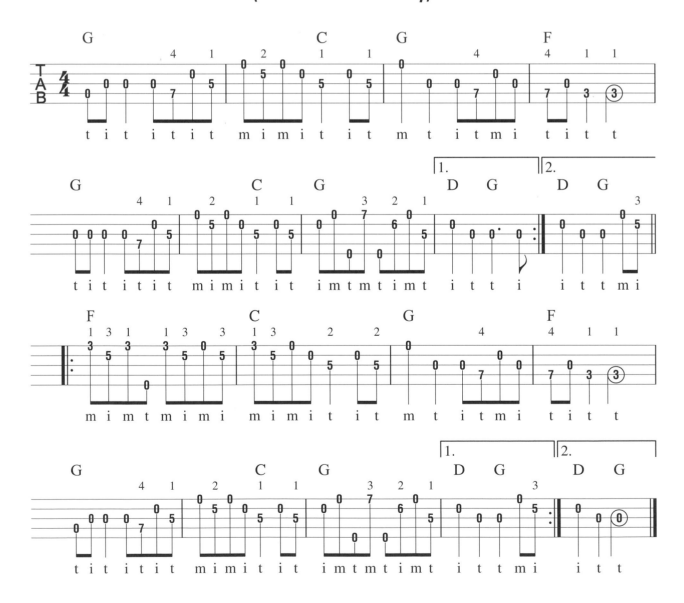

"The Sailor's Hornpipe" was first introduced to bluegrass audiences by a banjo player named Bill Keith. This tune and "The Devil's Dream" were among the first tunes to be played in melodic style. The term "Keith style" is sometimes used to identify melodic playing.

THE SAILOR'S HORNPIPE

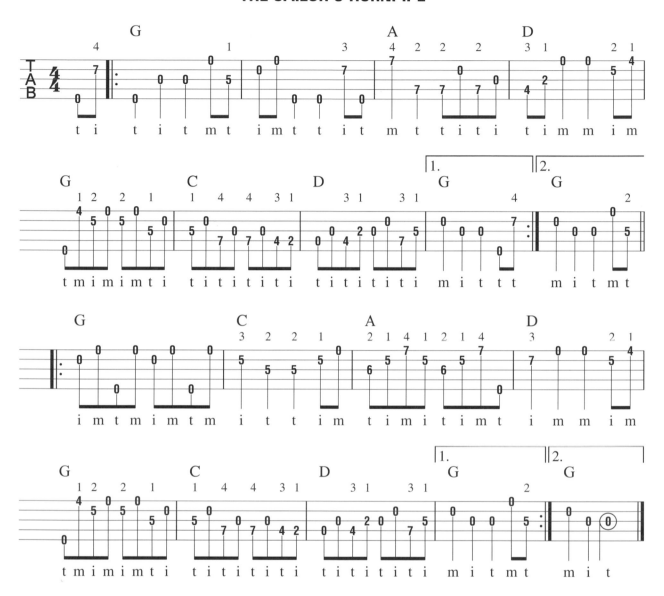

Can you play an appropriate back-up part for "The Sailor's Hornpipe" using these chord forms?

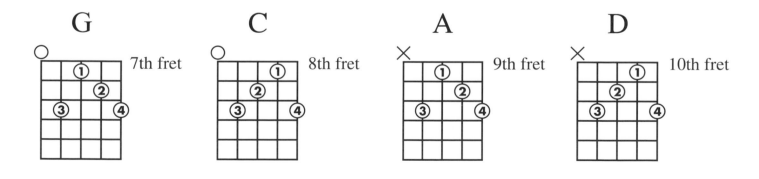

UNDERSTANDING CHORDS

A **chord** is sounded when several notes are played simultaneously. Most chords you have played have been stacks of three notes in the following relationship (using every other note of a scale):

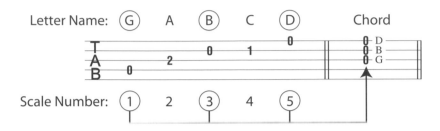

Chords are named for their lowest note, called the **root**. Below are the chords built on the first (I), fourth (IV), and fifth (V) notes of the G major scale:

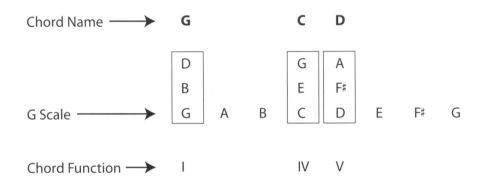

The Roman numeral is used to indicate the chord function within the key. The I, IV, and V chords are the most commonly used chords in most songs. In the key of C the I, IV, and V chords would be:

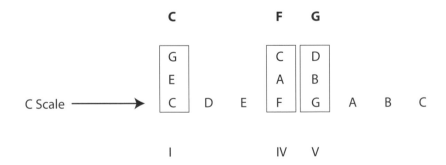

When you play a chord on the banjo you often double some of the chord tones, that is, the same letter name is played on more than one string.

TRANSPOSITION CHART

You already know how to raise a song from G to A or B by using a capo (see page 58).

If you find a song in a key such as D or F and wish to transpose it to G, you must learn to substitute chords according to their function. Below is a chart to help you. Follow these steps when using the chart:

- Find the key of the song you want to transpose by locating the last note and final chord. (This works 99% of the time.)

- Locate the chords on the chart in the original key.

- Move up the columns to the key of G and substitute the chords found there.

TRANSPOSITION CHART

Common Keys	Chord Functions		
	I	IV	V*
G	G	C	D(7)
F	F	B♭	C(7)
E	E	A	B(7)
E♭	E♭	A♭	B♭(7)
D	D	G	A(7)
C	C	F	G(7)
B	B	E	F#(7)
B♭	B♭	E♭	F(7)
A	A	D	E(7)

* The added seventh (7) is optional on the V chords.

CHORD CHART

COMMON CHORDS FOR BANJO IN G TUNING

"X" indicates fifth string is silent

"O" indicates fifth string is part of chord

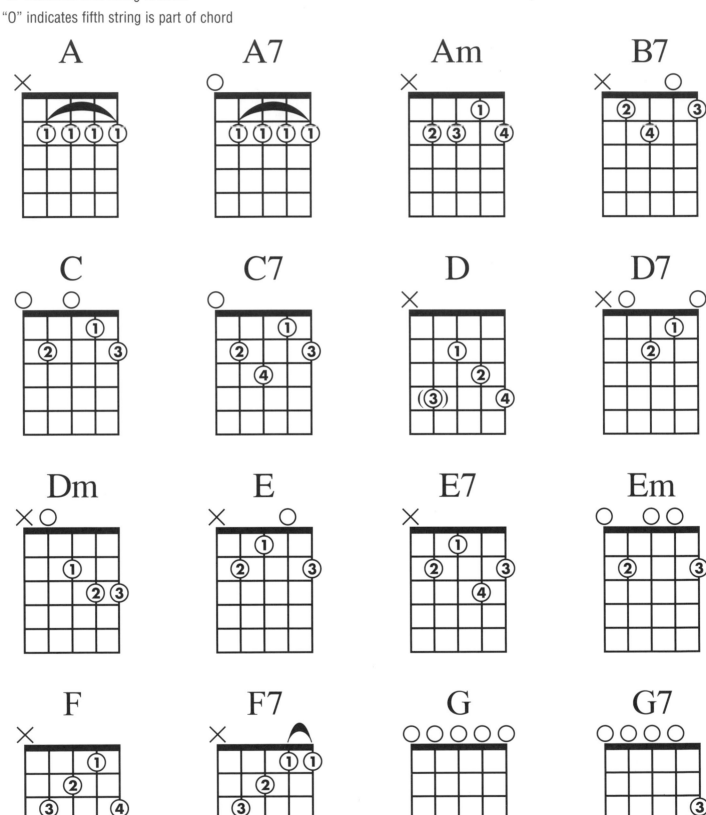